GOOD MARRIAGES DON'T JUST HAPPEN

GOOD MARRIAGES DON'T JUST HAPPEN

*For those who have a good marriage
and want to keep it
and those who do not but wish they did.*

O. Dean Martin

Fleming H. Revell Company
Old Tappan, New Jersey

Excerpts from YOUR INNER CHILD OF THE PAST copyright © 1963
by W. Hugh Missildine. Reprinted by permission of Simon & Schuster, a
division of Gulf & Western Corporation.
Lyrics from MY WOMAN, MY WOMAN, MY WIFE by Marty Robbins
used by permission of MARIPOSA MUSIC, INC. © 1969.

Library of Congress Cataloging in Publication Data
Martin, O. Dean (Oliver Dean), date
   Good marriages don't just happen
   1. Marriage.   2. Marriage—Religious aspects—
Christianity.   I. Title.
HQ734.M4272   1984   646.7′8   83-13901
ISBN 0-8007-1377-X

TO Sandra

Contents

Preface

Good Marriages Don't Just Happen is written for couples who have a good marriage and want to keep it that way and for singles or pairs who do not, but wish they did. The focus of the book is on three basic themes: (1) the unique characteristics to be found in relationships that are healthy and happy; (2) the idea that healthy relationships will not automatically continue unaided; and (3) practical guidelines for the care and maintenance of a good marriage.

We do not find the right person and then live happily ever after! We find the person right for us and then we must consciously do the things that preserve and advance the partnership. The guidelines in this book could be applied as well to the care and maintenance of any good thing: a great car, good house, good health, faith, job, and so forth. Everything good or great requires the same tender loving care. The focus of the book, however, will be on the care and maintenance of a good marriage.

This study is the natural evolution of my own conscious effort to keep my good marriage of twenty-six years headed for the better. It also incorporates my work for twenty-five years with couples of all types, sizes, shapes, and backgrounds—in their troubles and heartaches. I have been of considerable help to many of these couples and many of them have been of great help to me. We all need objectivity and perspective and, thus, often the counselor becomes the counselee.

Hundreds upon hundreds of couples have helped me redefine the meaning of courage and discover again the importance of patience, persistence, and tenacity. They have shown me living examples of what is wrong and destructive in a relationship. They have been my teachers as to what is right and constructive. I have seen them every hour of the day and most hours of the night.

During one three-year period I saw, and limited myself to, twenty couples per week. Along with what was in reality a full counseling load, I was also the senior minister of a large and very active church. I was actually attempting to do two to three full-time jobs. Finally, my body went on strike. I assumed I was only burning the

9

candle at both ends, but that candle turned out to be a stick of dyna-
mite and I became incapacitated for about three months. The
church staff carried the Kingdom, while God had to rough it without me.

When I began to come out of the fog, I still wanted to help in the
field of marriage counseling but knew it would have to be on a new
and different level. I felt, and still feel, such agony for the truly fine
marriages going down the drain all about us. Most of these
breakups were and are so unnecessary. They are but abdications of
the normal maturation process, generally to be resumed in another
marriage—and that no easier than the first.

A surprisingly few practical guidelines and perspectives had
helped me so much, I determined to share these with openness and
decided on some sort of small group setting with several couples at a
time, rather than just one. I thoroughly prepared my presentations,
based on my own experiences and vulnerabilities and borrowing,
always, only from the very best sources. I announced the small-
group seminar and about five hundred people attended each session! I was surprised at the response. I knew my mother would think
the material wonderful and helpful, but it took awhile to absorb the
notion that so many others found it practical and meaningful.

I shared the material again the following fall, with about the
same number of people, and then taught it as a course at the University of Florida the following year. The church I serve in Gainesville, Florida, received requests for several thousand copies of the
lectures. The series was subsequently filmed at United Methodist
Communications studios in Nashville, Tennessee. This book is the
latest development in the process.

In this study I deliberately use simple terms and illustrations to
state highly complex issues. I want this work to be clear enough for
any reader to say either, "I see what you are saying and I accept it"
or "I see that and I do not accept it." I do not write to protect myself
from experts in the field but to help those plowing in the field. I try
to help by communicating clearly and by illustrating simply.

Care and maintenance does not involve rebuilding an automatic
transmission but knowing when and how to check the points and
plugs!

O. DEAN MARTIN
GAINESVILLE, FLORIDA

GOOD MARRIAGES
DON'T JUST HAPPEN

CHAPTER 1

Why Good Marriages Go Bad:
The Two E's

We know why bad marriages go bad. They are simply bad. No one expects them to survive. That couple should not have gotten married in the first place! We always knew they wouldn't make it.

But, what really is frightening and surprising to us today is how many really *good marriages* are going down the tube. It is all a little scary and disconcerting. They seemed so stable! They appeared so much in love! They had so much going for them! They are our friends of long standing at the office, in our respectable neighborhood, even down at the church, and sometimes even are "our minister and his lovely wife."

We are seeing so many of these good marriages fail that the sheer volume suggests an epidemic. It *isn't* an epidemic, but failure certainly is no longer unusual. If nothing else, the data serves to remind us that good marriages can go bad and that no one is immune. The evidence also disputes the myth that good marriages do not fail and boldly raises two basic questions: "Why is this happening?" and "What can be done to safeguard a healthy marriage?" These are the two primary questions that constitute the focal point of this book. They need and deserve our undivided attention because good marriages do go bad, and, in fact, most bad marriages are good marriages gone bad! There are reasons for this, and there is preventive maintenance available.

Perhaps we can begin to approach the heart of the problem of the breakdown of a good relationship by exploring the naive supposition that a good union is always and eternally equated with "happiness ever after." The assumption goes something like this: "If I can just find Miss Right, that divine, wonderful angel . . ." "If I can just find Mr. Wonderful, that macho, gentle beast . . ." If and when we discover and claim the *right person,* we tend to believe—and heaven knows we've been taught—that married life is all automatic from that point on. We shall indeed live happily ever after.

This particular view of marriage is about as logical as saying, "If I can just get a beautiful new car that isn't a lemon, that has all the 'goodies' on it that I have always wanted, then it will be smooth sailing from then on." Or, "If I can just get a good, well-built, quality house, I'll never have to worry about it again." If it's great and good, it's not supposed to require care and maintenance. It will go on and on even though we do nothing. So begins our neglect.

We all want something that is top quality, which survives and thrives on neglect! This is what we want in a job, a house, a car, faith, flowers, health, and happiness. We want something that is so good that it automatically generates its own sustenance. This is *why* good cars and good houses and good marriages often go bad! *Everything good requires care and maintenance!* "Even if marriages are made in heaven, man has to be responsible for the maintenance!"*

Before I proceed further, let me define "good marriage." In a good marriage your partner gives you enough to make them worth living with despite their normal quota of negative attributes. Put another way, *everyone* is hard to live with! A good marriage is when your partner gives you enough to make it worth putting up with the natural negatives *everyone* brings to *any* marriage!

I also define good marriage as being *high majority positive.* Let me illustrate. I recently overheard a member of my congregation speaking with a mutual friend. She was expressing high majority positive in the following statement: "Today is our twenty-fifth wedding anniversary! These have been twenty-three great years!" That is high majority positive. For me, on the occasion of the twenty-fifth anniversary of our good marriage, I could say it has been twenty-three and one-half great years (for my wife I estimate

---

* Reprinted with permission from the *Alma* [Ga.] *Times* and the November 1979 *Reader's Digest.*

twenty-four!). You will seldom, if ever, do better than twenty-three and one-half (or twenty-four) out of twenty-five.

Everyone is hard to live with. Even when Miss/Mr. Right is found, there will be a day here, a week there, three weeks in another year, a month the next year, two hours here, and two days there when you will want to push them off the second story and tell God they tripped! This is normal, natural, and predictable. You have a good marriage when you are receiving and giving enough to carry each other through these natural and inevitable periods of unpleasantness. A good marriage is when you experience high majority positive!

Finally, before going on to the remainder of this chapter, a more specific exploration of why good can go bad, and the subsequent chapters describing what can be done about it (care and maintenance), let me caution you not to pass me or fail me on the basis of religious test words. Please do not evaluate these contents on whether the material is "spiritual" enough. I, in turn, shall not presume to give you a graduation plaque stating in chalky eloquence: "The Family That Prays Together Stays Together."

I believe deeply in faith and praying together and staying together and the Bible! I just think the complex problem of why good marriages do go bad must be addressed without being limited to a single discipline or to quick, simple solutions.

I have found, for instance, that faith does not negate or neutralize neurosis. Faith *does* give us more incentive, more willingness and strength, to face our neurosis meaningfully, but faith does not do away with our personal needs.

My understanding of faith has been summarized, at least in part, by someone who said: "Faith makes things possible, not easy." We all want a faith that makes things easy! Of course! Why not? We are far more realistic, however, when we seek a faith that motivates and enables.

Having offered my definition of good marriage and having solicited your understanding of the importance and the place of faith, let me explore the four most-common causal factors in the demise of good marriages. These unique problems must be identified, isolated, and treated.

In this chapter we will cover the two "E's": energy and expectation.

Energy

The first of these unique problems is *energy*. A good marriage simply has more energy, more dynamic, more fire than does a weak marriage. There is obviously more energy in a meteoric marriage than will ever be found in a mediocre marriage. Or, look at the pervasive détente relationships of our day. When a couple lives together in mutual distrust, cold war, or simply resigned tolerance, there is not much steam in the relationship. But when we love and are loved; when we work and strive; when the marriage is good; energy is present! And, energy is capable of building up OR burning down; it can create or destroy; propel or consume.

Today the fashionable word that characterizes this initial problem unique to good marriages is *burnout*. The implication of *burnout* is that we experience too much of a good thing, that energy is not controlled or maintained.

Burnout does not come from overwork or from being trapped in a job or relationship we do not enjoy. Burnout comes from being fortunate enough to be involved in an experience we love or enjoy *so much* that we carelessly fail to vary the routine. The job or relationship is so fulfilling, stimulating, or rewarding that we compulsively pursue its regimen with little or no awareness of the dangers involved in playing with fire. One day the energy that is inherent in this enjoyable situation spreads on its own into wildfire. Energy, that kind unique to good situations, needs proper care and deliberate maintenance. If this does not occur, the circuit melts and we experience brownout or, worse, blackout. One day we simply wake up to the awareness that we no longer feel what we once did about the job, the hobby, the marriage. Energy can create or destroy. Good situations have the unique problem of burnout potential.

In his autobiography Harry Emerson Fosdick shared the story of a nervous breakdown he suffered while serving his first church. He used a most interesting sentence to summarize this experience. Dr. Fosdick said, "I was slain by joy." He loved his job, and without letup or change he pursued this love. We do not tend to realize or appreciate this enigma. We think we are always slain by misery when, more often than not, we are cut down by joy!

This high energy level generated by good experiences can be found in any area of life. For instance, a personal example concerns my interest in football. I once watched every game on television.

Football was my break from the harsh realities of human suffering. I was truly and deeply thankful I had something I enjoyed so much, something that gave me break time and a chance to recharge my own energies. I never varied my routine; I simply enjoyed my good fortune. Then, one day I awakened to find this unchecked and unvaried energy had caused brownout. Today my interest in football is pretty well confined to what the University of Florida Gators are doing, plus some lingering interest in the Miami Dolphins.

I am presently engaged in reviving my interest in football, but am using the energy generated by this good relationship more wisely. I am no longer allowing it to burn away at *one* point but am broadening that interest into creative activities such as interest in players I know, working with a team as chaplain, and so forth.

This is, in fact, the answer to the unique problem of energy and burnout: Vary the ritual; avoid sameness at all costs; expand the scope of your involvement. My pastoral job, for instance, was recently reinvigorated by following this advice. I am prone to working seven days a week at my job because I dearly love my work. I found myself in my office all day, every day, and this was slowly creating staleness. What I did was very simple and effective. I moved my Saturday work to my study at the house and stayed out of the office at the church for at least one full day each week. That simple move really helped! It will need more variation and further improvement later but is effective for now.

In the same way, my marriage has been helped by doing some things differently from time to time and scrupulously avoiding sameness. It is easy to let good things run on until the rut is so deep that one feels smothered and burned out. I will speak of this solution in more detail in chapter three. For now, remember that good marriages have more energy than do bad or mediocre relationships, and the higher the energy level, the greater the potential AND the danger! Good marriages, like good jobs and good hobbies, go bad because unusual energy is present and is taken for granted rather than constantly being reevaluated and creatively channeled.

Expectation

A second basic reason good marriages often go bad is *expectation.* We certainly expect much from a good thing. And the better a thing is the more it tempts us to expect much from it! This normal expectation, generated uniquely by the good, must constantly be tempered by reality and preserved by our ability to adjust.

Such was the case of the young man who determined that his first vehicle would be the epitome of his dreams. He worked and saved, dreamed and toiled, until the fateful day arrived when he purchased this dream machine. It was a beautiful van—loaded, luxurious, and as good as they come, the perfection of the engineer and designer's art. The young man had every right to expect a great deal from this mechanical marvel. He bought the vehicle and drove it off the lot with the pride and aura of a man who knows destiny and determination have conspired to bring about the perfect union.

The next day, however, the beautiful new van was towed, bent and battered, back to the dealership. An angry and disillusioned owner stormed into the office of the salesman, not only demanding a complete refund, but also threatening to sue for medical damages.

"What happened?" asked the startled salesman.

"I bought your van," the young man sputtered. "I drove it out to the interstate to give it a test run. I set the automatic cruise control, went to the back to fix myself a cup of coffee, and the darn thing ran off the road!"

This apocryphal story serves to remind us that expectation minus a sense of reality and void of adjustment skills often equal disaster! The problem is not the quality of the match up, but rather the fact that the match is so good, so perfect, that preconceptions and expectations tend to run wild. This is one of the peculiar and unique problems of truly good marriages. It is one of the unique problems of truly good anything. Nobody expects much from a poor or mediocre job, but we logically expect much, perhaps too much, from a good or great job. Good marriages, like good anything, often stagger under the awesome load of high expectation.

This phenomenon of high expectation usually finds expression in two basic desires: (1) We expect continuation of the good things we received from our loved ones in our early childhood and (2) *simultaneously,* we expect our partner to correct the hurts, fill the vacuums, and alleviate the pains that still haunt us from our childhood. These expectations are usually conflicting and *hidden agenda* (concerns or expectations not openly stated). We have a right to expect much from a good match up but not the right to expect these two things to happen simultaneously and without creative conflict.

I am as good a case study for illustrating this phenomenon as is anyone drawn from the files of a marriage clinic. I was born a spoiled brat and very early in life experienced a relapse! I came into the world as a mid-life accident. Not only that—I had three sisters and no brothers. In effect, I had four mothers and was an only child to all four! I not only felt great love and security in my home, but all five of us considered me special and, while not perfect, at least one whose faults should be overlooked and of whom nothing should be required and very little expected.

When I went away to college and began in earnest the search for my new mother (my wife), I wanted someone who could (1) give me all the love and affection to which I was accustomed, but who would somehow, simultaneously and unbeknown to me, (2) help me develop into a mature and responsible adult! These needs are loaded with conflict and contradiction when pursued simultaneously and without awareness.

My wife and I, now beginning our second quarter century of marriage, are learning to be in touch with our expectations, to uncover the hidden agenda. We are watching these conflicting agenda and not allowing our hopes and dreams to be set on automatic cruise control! We are learning to control our expectations and not allow our expectations to control us.

When we, as happily married couples, allow our expectations to control us, we become disillusioned with each other. Then comes the option for crash and trade-in! Our society encourages this trade-in mentality, and our own penchant for the quick fix exacerbates this mind-set. To counter this, expectations must always be under the supervision and influence of reality.

Let me conclude this reflection on expectation, the second unique problem in good marriages, by stating the problem in rule form: All inspiration *institutionalizes.* This means that when we fall in love, find faith, feel anger, feel pity (any inspiration), we must place that feeling in a container or it fades and dies. The container (the institutionalization) could be getting married, joining a church, joining the air force, joining the Salvation Army, and so forth. Inspiration must be institutionalized in order to survive. If we are in love with someone, only marriage (institutionalization) will preserve that love!

In any institution in which I choose to nourish my inspiration there are easy times of growth and assimilation followed by predictable periods of struggle and trial. Nothing flows smoothly! I enjoy, but I must work for that enjoyment.

I call these predictable periods of pain or struggle that follow times of joy *maturation ceilings*. When we reach one of these ceilings, we must hang in there, pay the price, push on through, grow up a little. Thus we make the eternal discovery that there is another patch of joy just beyond that struggle. Maturation ceilings are the steps in the stairs pointing to the elusive penthouse!

Changing institutions does not compensate or facilitate! If I leave this marriage just because I want to avoid these necessary steps that require maturity and growth, I do myself a great injustice as well as those about me. I simply reencounter the very same maturation requirements in any subsequent marriage. Then they usually come sooner and more intensely. Let me illustrate.

When I lived in Miami some years ago, the *Herald* carried an intriguing series of stories on a subculture group camped out in the Coconut Grove area of the city. This group was in search of the *perfect* society. Perfect society can usually be translated as "something other than the one I am in that (1) gives me all the good I expect and (2) corrects the unacceptable without bothering me!" This was precisely the pursuit of this group.

In quest of their goal a small band of these young adults decided to remove themselves from their first society, their present imperfect government, and move into one of the huge tropical banyan trees in the grove. Here they proposed to create their own utopian society. They remained in the tree for approximately six ecstatic weeks. Then disillusionment set in again. They found that living together in this new society brought them face-to-face with the very same frustration and maturation needs experienced in the society that drove them into the tree. About half of them left. They built a third Utopia in the spreading branches of yet another banyan tree. In less than *three* weeks the procedure was repeated, and yet a fourth Utopia was established. Such a process is painful, unrealistic, and a waste of good energy—whether in a utopian society or in our quest for a perfect marriage.

We might just as well grow up some time and move willingly to face these maturation ceilings. It is important to deal with our penchant for nonthreatening or nondemanding solutions. If not, we inevitably encounter the same point of frustration that defeated us in our last relationship. Only this time, we meet it sooner and with more intensity.

It is because of our quick-fix, nondisciplined reaction to frustrations that I habitually have to tell the man who periodically comes to my office, to think twice before he trades "banyan trees." I encourage him to make a good marriage out of the one he's got, because each subsequent attempt introduces the same conflicts sooner and usually with less ability to cope. I have said many times, "I understand why you want to leave your wife for your secretary. I have seen your secretary, and your wife is as old as you are! But, make the marriage you've got beautiful before you bail out. You are going to *have* to face your real problems sooner or later anyway. You may find you are where you ought to be, with the person you ought to be with—and just think of the alimony you can save!"

Of course, divorce will always be with us, but divorce is often an effort to go around a problem. It is usually a solution and not an answer. It tends to obscure the reality that in a *good* faith, in a *good* job, in a *good* marriage there are rewarding and easy times, followed by times requiring that we grow up. And, we might just as well hang in there, *grow up,* and save all that grief and alimony!

Louise Montague writes about this problem with considerable insight:

> ... Divorce is a solution for one problem only: an unworkable marriage. It is not a remedy for an unhappy job situation, the restlessness of middle age, or self-dislike. People who divorce because of an *extraneous* problem often find that they have not only failed to solve the problem, they have also separated themselves from the *one person* who might have been of genuine help.

Fra Giovanni, in 1513, said it in yet another way: "No peace lies in the future which is not hidden in the present." That is true for *most* of us.

Again, the second most prevalent problem of truly good marriages is *expectation.* Good marriages cause us to expect so much. We must be in touch with and in control of this tendency.

CHAPTER 2

Why Good Marriages Go Bad: The Two P's

In chapter one I dealt with the two "E's" that represent problems unique to good marriages: *energy* and *expectation*. This chapter rounds out the "big four" with a look at the two "P's": *paradox* and *perspective*.

Paradox

The third basic causal factor in the demise of good marriages is *paradox*. Webster defines *paradox* as a statement or premise that seems contradictory.

Perhaps the greatest paradox of all is that good marriages *can* go bad. This is a premise or statement that certainly seems contradictory! We shall probably eternally assume that if the match is good, the pairing right, the chemistry correct, and the arrangement fell from the "divine computer bank in the sky," then it will be problem free! We shall probably always be disturbed and dismayed by the paradox that good is not automatically and constantly good.

Paradox, though it stands on this list as the third fundamental unique problem to be found in good marriages, has a list all its own. There is the paradox of self-competition, the equally disruptive paradox of attraction, and the paradox of guilt. We need to explore each of these.

It seems contradictory to say that we must compete with ourselves, yet that is the case. The higher we go in gratification and subsequent reward, the more hard pressed we are to accommodate lesser moments. This is the paradox of *self-competition*. Marriages that are exceptionally good have this unique bind. A good marriage, like a good golfer, a capable lecturer, a talented gardener, or a skilled athlete often has more difficulty competing with itself than with an outside pressure!

Put another way, an awareness of how good a marriage *can be* carries dangers no bad marriage *ever* faced. For instance, in a marriage whose *high* point could only be described as "blah," a couple is not so threatened or annoyed by normal down periods. But if, on the other hand, a marriage is quite accustomed to marvelous peak experiences in affection, companionship, physical exuberance, spiritual sensitivity, and so forth, there is far more trauma to be dealt with when normal off periods are experienced in the relationship.

This particular paradox is quite easily illustrated not just in marriage but whenever and wherever achievement and success are evident. For example, where I live, Southeastern Conference football is an integral part of the folk culture. I follow it with interest, as do many of my fellow southerners, though my interest is now somewhat less than life-or-death involvement. One of our SEC member schools is Vanderbilt University in Nashville, Tennessee. Our family lived in Nashville many years ago, and while there I came to appreciate the Vandy Commodores and attended as many games as I could. In those days, however, if someone *drove* by Dudley Field, near the Vandy campus, and blew their horn on Thursday before a game on Saturday, Vanderbilt felt they had experienced a good season. In those days "blah" was their zenith experience (though that is now drastically changing).

On the other hand, if at the University of Alabama, another SEC school, *one* game were to be lost during the regular season, denying Alabama the mythical national championship (and leaving them "just" winners of the SEC championship), they moaned and groaned for months! You would hear them saying such things as: "We had an off year," or, during coach Bear Bryant's lifetime, "The Bear's getting too old!" Great football teams, like great marriages that experience exhilarating heights, have more trouble working through normal down periods than do the mediocre ones.

Richard Farson of the Western Behavioral Sciences Institute says it this way:

> The better a marriage is the worse its partners will sometimes feel. It's a paradox we *must* learn to live with. . . . Couples lucky enough to have these moments are unable to sustain them and, at the same time, unable to settle for *ordinary* moments. They want life to be constantly satisfying. But to achieve a constant state, to avoid the valleys, it is necessary to eliminate the peaks, which put the marriage on a narrow band of involvement.

Good marriages experience this paradox. But, by understanding that it happens, we can learn to assimilate its existence and, in turn, find more courage to patiently and diligently break through our maturation thresholds into other good times.

A second dimension or illustration of the problem of paradox within a good marriage is the paradox of *attraction*. This example was alluded to earlier in the book under the heading of hidden and conflicting agenda but must be mentioned briefly in this context because it is blatant and unabashed paradox. It simply never occurs to us that the person who is truly right for us can be and must be a source of creative conflict. Perhaps we must cease defining "right for us" as someone who is the guardian of our comfort and happiness. When we have done this, we may soon come to see that a good match up is one where we are both loved and helped. This creative conflict to be found in truly good marriages was well captured by Dr. Richard Halverson when he said, "Good marriages are *forged*. They come by heat and hammer."

If you have a good marriage, you actually are in for the heat and the hammer pushing you toward the grand design. You will know melting, molding, and maturation. In short, you will experience the paradox of a truly good marriage. You will know love and help, peace and propelling friction.

There is at least one other major paradox to be found in good marriages. It is the paradox of *guilt*. Do not interpret guilt in the narrow sense of the term. That is, when we hear the word, we tend to think of strong feelings indicating the presence of wrongdoing. Not so, *most* of the time. Guilt, fully the majority of the time, does not indicate wrongdoing but sensitivity and awareness.

I observed this paradox in action the other evening when I decided to forego my pastoral responsibilities in order to spend an evening with my wife (and I do this regularly!). That evening, as we sat in the den enjoying a quiet evening together, I felt rather guilty that I was not out calling. I could think of two or three specific families who needed my attention and who could be helped by my simply being interested enough to call. The next evening I went out calling only to discover, for the umpteenth time, that I felt a little guilty because I was not at home with my wife!

Guilt sometimes does, of course, indicate wrongdoing, but most of the time it simply indicates that we are sensitive and caring people. In fact, people who *are* doing wrong things often feel no guilt at all. And, conversely, those with broad horizons and deep compassions who are bending every effort to be of use to our society often feel guilty. It is in this broader dimension that guilt enters good marriages in the form of paradox.

The classic illustration of this phenomenon, especially as it is manifested in middle-class America, goes something like this. When things are good, when we are in love, happy, secure, and know it, we tend to seek out problems or make mountains out of molehills in order to maintain equilibrium with the mad, decaying world about us. *Because* we have it so good, many of our families seek out little problems and blow them all out of proportion. Thus, we generate the feeling that our family shares the common agony. Everyone about us seems to be in some conflict or peril; we are kind and sensitive and want to carry our fair share of the burdens of life—so we create our own. This is a peril of good, blessed, stable marriages. We must learn to live with superficial guilt.

We do not usually perceive this reaction as a form of guilt. After all, guilt tells us something is wrong, therefore we must identify it and correct the wrong. The tendency to disrupt the good because so much about us is bad is guilt also. When things are good, and the world is so full of bad; when our life is relatively smooth sailing and storms are crashing all about us; when nothing truly horrendous exists within our marriage or family to occupy our time or release our guilt; we will respond by finding or creating something that is bad. I think this dynamic was in part what Horatius Bonar was thinking about when he said over 100 years ago, "Mankind can survive anything except continual prosperity."

The healthy and creative solution to this particular paradox is to recognize and affirm the fact that we are sensitive, aware, and caring human beings. We must reach out to others *in* our own secure and happy situation and not take the tempting road of joining the confusion about us by subconsciously finding fault and insecurity in our marriage in order to feel less guilty.

As someone prayed so eloquently, "Lord, give me the grace to live with my blessings." Good marriages must learn how to live with paradox. This could be the paradox of competing with one's own peak experiences. Or, it could be the paradox of the creative conflict inherent in why we are subconsciously attracted to someone. Or, we may need to live with the paradox of learning to live with grace, poise, and thanksgiving in a secure and stable relationship.

Perspective

Good marriages do have unique problems! These problems must be assessed and assimilated if the union is to remain meaningful. We come now to the fourth of the big four—*perspective.*

It is precisely *because* the relationship is good and we are not preoccupied with patching leaks in the boat or frantically bailing water that we can look about us on the lake and notice what a great sailor everyone else seems to be! We, because of lack of perspective, view theirs and judge ours by the proverbial, "The water is always bluer on the other side."

Illustrating this fourth principle comes easily from the experience my wife and I have had with our marriage as well as through my work with the marriages of others. Over the years I have scrupulously maintained strict confidence when working with other couples in their deeply private struggles. As close as my wife and I are, I have never revealed either the occasion or the content of a counseling situation. We both prefer this, and the pattern has been followed for twenty-five years.

Because of this mutual arrangement, however, I have been exposed to some interesting observations relative to the problem of perspective. From time to time, like any other healthy and happy couple, we go through periods in our marriage that are strained, discouraging, or even hostile (after all, she isn't ordained and therefore is not as easy to live with as I am). My wife has said to me on two or three such occasions, "Why can't we be like so-and-so? They hold hands, look so in love, seem so close." On many occasions when I have heard her, or other distraught wives express this pleading wish, I have spent weeks, or *am* spending weeks, with that very couple trying to help them hold their marriage together! This is what I mean by perspective.

Richard W. Farson put it this way, "If we really could know more about other people's marriages, we would see that they are much more similar than different—painfully, hilariously, reassuringly alike."

Stop for just a moment and give the picture some real thought! Can we not rather easily see that *often* a marriage LOOKS its best when the couple is actually trying their hardest to save it? Does that really sound so illogical? Can we not readily see that a perspective that encompasses this paradox could be of much help in our own marriage?

Often we are looking at a couple who are in trouble. They do not want to be in trouble or do not want you to know they are—or both! They hold hands, extend dating courtesies (more on that important subject, dating courtesies, in chapter six), gaze lovingly at one another, and walk about arm in arm. The marriage LOOKS great. And, may be. But my point here is that many times couples look their best when they are, in fact, trying hardest to save the marriage.

Interestingly, as I was working on this chapter, a friend of mine asked me about a couple known to both of us who had recently divorced. He said, "I can't understand it! The last time I saw them they were walking through the lobby of a hotel just being as lovey-dovey as you please. You would have thought they were the most in-love people on earth!" I knew the couple much better than he, and I responded, "They've been trying to save that marriage for twenty years. What you saw were two nice people in the last desperate throes of a relationship, who were mutually unwilling to throw in the sponge until the very last breath."

This observation that couples often look their best when they are trying hardest to save the relationship should not, of course, be carried too far. Any couple caught holding hands should not immediately be categorized as on their last legs! And, when it *is* the case that they are struggling, we should be aware that they are not primarily trying to deceive others or themselves. They are primarily trying to reassure each other, make a resolute effort, and *act* themselves into a new way of thinking. But, to the casual observer they look so stable, so much in love.

We need perspective! We need the kind of overview that enables us to appreciate our own unique marriage, while leaving others to enjoy or work through theirs. We must always keep perspective. Simply speaking, perspective is a problem unique to *good* marriages because only *good* marriages offer us the time and security that enable us to be so preoccupied with other people's marriages! A couple in a bad marriage are so busy bailing out their own boat that they are not doing much sightseeing. Only those in good marriages tend to lose perspective. Only good marriages afford that kind of time and energy!

These first two chapters have been an effort to make more obvious the subtle reality that good marriages can and do go down the drain. *Just like* good jobs, good cars, and good houses they can fall into lethal disrepair! This dynamic is not inevitable in everything good but is predictable in the absence of proper care and maintenance. The proper care and maintenance of a good marriage is the essence of the chapters to follow.

We have heard it said that building a good marriage is similar to building a good fire. There is the initial blaze with its flame and beauty. The paper and kindling quickly burn down. You fan the flames and hope and your eyes get teary from blinding smoke. You wonder if all is not lost. You keep giving it time and attention. Finally, the big log catches. So, too, can a carefully tended relationship move into a warmer, richer dimension. Subsequent chapters seek to explore *how* to kindle and hope—how to give time and attention to that good marriage.

CHAPTER 3

Identifying the "Little You"

We all bring into our marriage all the "little people" we ever were. Every little boy or every little girl we ever were is still part of us, consciously or subconsciously. They are filed away in our memory bank and are regularly or irregularly activated by the things that go on about us in our adult world. This is the principle of the *little you* or the *inner child* of the past.

Martin Buber, the noted Jewish philosopher, called this "the is-ness of the was," the "wasness of the is." We *are* part of what we always were. What we *were* still affects what we are.

Practically speaking, we can say that when we reach physical maturity, we all have two basic personalities struggling for dominance inside our adult mind. We could call these our domestic personality and our social personality.

The *domestic personality* is the little child, our previous experiences, still inside us. It is the person we are when we do not think, watch our step, or consciously control our inner child. We tend to become what our child dictates, and as a result, we don't apply our social skills.

Our *social personality* is the person we are when we are in touch with our past. Being in touch we use our brain, watch our step, guard against the doing of "what comes naturally." The social personality is not automatic but is the we, we must *work* at becoming. This personality is the one we present in courtship and, therefore, the one that is apparent at the time of marriage.

This is precisely why people are often so very different after marriage. Before marriage they *work* at being the social person they *want* to be. Therefore, their social personality dominates. After marriage, they stop working at it and, often by default, allow their domestic personality to dominate. This is what Peter DeVries meant when he said, "The whole thing about matrimony is this: We fall in love with a personality, but we must live with a character."

To learn to control the domestic personality, our lingering child, and enhance the social personality, our preferred view of ourselves, is the essence of this chapter and the next. To allow the person we married to remain married to the person they fell in love with—this is why we must learn to identify and control the inner child.

Many of these inner children require little or no control because they are some of the best assets we bring to our marriage. When activated by stimuli in the present, these "healthy children" endow us with little-boy happiness or little-girl excitability. They make us fresh and alive. They make us trustingly innocent and creatively energetic. These healthy children, still within us, only need our affirmation and appreciation.

It is our "unhealthy children" within, their presence and impact, that is the focus of this chapter. These children cause us to feel offended, irritable, domineering, or perhaps sad. They may make us feel unduly aggressive or jealous. It is these children, the ones that cause so much unaccountable disruption in our marriage, that we need to recognize and control.

Many times, through being ignored or denied, the negative emotions caused by the inner child may appear without just cause. They can disrupt or even destroy a marriage. We know very well that things are not right in the relationship but do not know why. If the cause of difficulty is not apparent to *us,* how can it be to our husband or wife? Thus, these inner children can and often do cause irreparable damage in a marriage, with both partners having no idea of what precisely is responsible for all their misery.

The presence of these little boys and girls has been called many things: the inner child of the past, stored tapes in your computer bank, roots of personality, sources of temperament traits, separation therapy, our pathological dimension (more on that later), or as one author calls it, Big You-Little You. Whatever it is called, we must come to working terms with the fact that every little person we ever were is in us somewhere.

Hugh Missildine, a researcher who has done perhaps the most creative work in this area, says in *Your Inner Child of the Past:*

> Whether we like it or not, we are not just adults living wholly in the present. We are also the children we once were, still living with some, even much, of the home atmosphere, the emotional environment in which we were raised. We think we have outgrown the past but we have not. We were exposed to parental attitudes, perhaps all of them well intended, but not all of them valid and truly applicable to us. . . . They very much impinged on our lives as children; we developed certain attitudes and reactions in response to them. The child within us has not died. Nor have the attitudes, the good and the bad.

From my own marriage and the many marriages I have worked with over the years I have come to believe that the single most creative force, for good or bad, in marriage is this remnant of our past. This is largely because this presence is so hidden and subtle. It is hidden and subtle because most of us have not identified the presence and taken charge of its ramifications. Using Hugh Missildine's term, the inner child of the past, when identified and controlled, can also be the making of a good marriage!

We can deny that this really has anything to do with our marriage. We can vigorously exclaim, as do many people, "I live in the *present!* I do not want to talk about my childhood! That's not going to help me now!" But we still do not do away with the reality.

The anguish behind these denials is both understandable and obvious. We tend to feel this way when there are things we would like to forget or pretend never occurred.

By trying to run away from these children, however, and denying their input into our present lives, we but run into their arms. We leave them in charge of us when we could be in control of them. We can identify and govern them so that they can help our marriage, both the good children as well as the negative and disruptive. But by denial or poor identification, we are doing two things. We are not allowing the full development of the good child and, by abdication, we are leaving the bad child to rule our marriage.

These children are there and we've got to come to grips with this fact! As an anonymous author has written: "We never grow up, so it seems. We keep in our hearts all our dreams, and in a corner we find, tucked away, the child we all were yesterday."

The trick is to call him or her out of the corner. Talk to the child.

Raise and nurture the child. And, if nothing else, govern and discipline that specific negative child. In this way the child can become a constructive force within our selves and, thus, in our marriage relationship.

Before exploring the idea that the child can be a constructive force in our marriage, let me delve into this principle a little further by discussing the word *pathology*. Pathology is a technical, clinical term, and its exploration may help us get a little more in touch with the whole process of identifying the inner-child principle. It will also help us in understanding its effect on our adult relationships, in general; and specifically, a practical understanding of the term can help us with the care and maintenance of a good marriage.

The word *pathology* is derived from two Greek words: *pathos,* which means suffering, and *logos,* which means speech. Thus, one's pathology in this case is the pain or hurt stored in the memory bank that is awakened by some external stimuli and is now speaking forth in the marriage.

Although general application of pathology cannot be explored in this book, we need to be aware that our "pain-speaking" inner child is pervasive in all of our adult relationships. This lingering presence speaks to and gives perspective in *every* adult relationship we pursue. It affects our perception of job, self, sport, recreation, faith, what is healthy or unhealthy, what is reality and nonreality in *all* of life. Marriage is but one of the more obvious dimensions in which we see the inner-child reality. It affects all of our adult relationships as well.

It is important also to realize that the pain-speaking inner child can be brought into our adult relationships, including marriage, from good childhood experiences as well as from bad ones. In fact, psychological bruises or scars can be even more difficult to handle when emanating from good homes. This is because love, sacrifice, and caring tend to dissipate our objectivity.

If, for instance, your mother beat you with a beer bottle, it becomes easier for you to say, "My mother was crazy but I loved her." On the other hand, if your parents directed you with manipulative love, or with guilt, you could be in trouble and not be fully aware of it. When people love us and care about us and give us their best, we are rather handicapped in our ability to scrutinize critically their negative contributions to our life.

I often tell people, "If your parents loved you and took you to church, you may have been ruined!" This is, of course, a facetious statement. Fundamentally, it means that even if one is so fortunate as to have received such assets as a love and faith orientation, these can be liabilities *if* we do not recognize that all parents represent both healthy and unhealthy role models. The assets become liabilities when they cripple our capacities for objective analysis of our past. It is open and honest awareness of the past that we need in order to keep the social personality developing and keep the hurting inner child in check.

Whether you call it pathology, the inner child, or whatever, we must recognize the reality of this principle. The child we all were yesterday is still tucked away in a corner somewhere! We must learn how to identify that child. We must learn how that particular child may be affecting our marriage. Case studies can be of some benefit in this pursuit.

How the Inner Child Works

These are actual cases, recounted to help the reader understand the principle of the inner child. Each is a study of this child at work in an unrecognized, and thus uncontrolled, state. It is important to bear in mind that these stories, while true, are simplistic and are chosen for that purpose. They allow the principle of the inner child to stand out in bold relief.

They are not meant to indicate that all children are easily subdued or directed. No implication is intended that easy and conspicuous answers exist for any and all personality problems. The intent of each example is but to illustrate clearly and simply the reality and impact of the inner child in a marriage relationship.

The Case of the Programmed Crisis

A young housewife we shall call Karen came to my office virtually every October. Her marriage was eternally over and finished in that particular month. She didn't know why, but she no longer loved her husband and, worse, felt deep hostility toward him. This perennial siege, this every-October programmed crisis, would last until about the end of December. Then love and tranquillity would once again return to the marriage.

After several Octobers of this repetition Karen was finally induced to do some free-association rambling through her childhood. What turned up was fascinating as well as unbelievably helpful!

When she was four years of age, she received a beautiful little cocker spaniel for her birthday. A few weeks after she got the puppy, Cinder was run over and killed in front of the house. The date was mid-October. The day was cool, dark, and rainy.

Her father, the special person in her life, was engrossed in Saturday-afternoon college football on television. The little girl ran into the family room to ask him to come see about Cinder, then lying lifeless in the street. He replied, "Yes, Honey. Just as soon as they make this touchdown, Daddy will be right there." Cinder died before "they" made their touchdown and would have died even if Karen and her father had gotten there earlier. But try telling that to a four-year-old child.

The adult Karen now carries the four-year-old Karen around in her eternal data bank. Every fall, when the weather turns cooler and cold drizzle begins to fall on an autumn afternoon saturated with college football, Karen feels neglected, forsaken, and deserted. Poor old Harold, her husband, who wasn't even the original culprit, gets paid back October after October for the wrong done the four-year-old still locked up and neglected inside Karen.

As far as Harold knows, he's simply enjoying a quiet afternoon at home watching a good college football game. Karen, however, is responding to unchecked and uncontrolled inner-child stimuli that are about to destroy her marriage.

Karen finally got in touch with what was happening. Realizing that it was Dad who had let her down and not Harold, she was better able to understand her feelings, the nature of her projection, and thus control and nourish her pain-speaking inner child. Before her awareness of the principle of the inner child, Karen was allowing the child to control her adult. Now she the adult is in charge of the child. For all practical purposes the programmed crisis of October is now in the process of being deprogrammed. Harold is enjoying football, and Karen is enjoying Harold—even in October!

How often do we do this kind of thing in our marriage? Far more often than we might suspect, though to lesser or stronger degrees and in varying degrees of awareness. We often project or transfer our feelings or hurts to other, inappropriate persons. This is almost always to our own detriment. It is particularly easy to do in marriage, where husbands replace fathers, wives replace mothers. Our domestic personality finds itself within a domestic setting, where it is so easy just to do its thing!

Words May Break My Bones

This story is from my own life. It is used because it aptly illustrates one of the more common areas where our pathology disrupts our marriage—the words from early childhood that fall on us like stones.

I grew up with an aversion to cigarettes. My aversion bordered on true paranoia. As a young boy and young adult I was simply terrified when someone tried to hand me one. I clearly remember taking a swing at a high school friend who attempted to make me take a cigarette. Strange!

To this very day I have never smoked a cigarette. I used to wonder why I felt the way I did and was quite bothered by being so "different."

But today, at age forty-eight, I am neither bothered by being different nor frightened by the presence of cigarettes. Some years ago, at thirty-two, I stumbled on the cause of my adult fear. Having discovered my particular inner child causing the paranoia, I am now free to smoke but smart enough not to start.

The cause of my deep fear began when I was *minus* two months old! While my mother was still carrying me, my brother, who was twelve at the time, accidentally shot himself. It seems he left our farm that fateful evening to spend the night with a friend. He was strictly forbidden to smoke. But, upon placing the barn between himself and the house, he began rolling a homemade cigarette. A passing neighbor saw him attempt to strike a match on the stock of his gun. He hit the trigger instead and the falling rifle discharged, killing him.

I was born months later. As my mother held me, she cried and told this story. As I grew into childhood, I continued to be exposed to this account. As a result, I had locked in my data bank the association of cigarettes with instant death. The words had fallen like stones and left me incapable of functioning normally in making my own objective choice.

Had I not made the discovery of this childhood causal factor, I would have continued to function in life, but with more pain. Now, while I see cigarettes as a slow, long-term killer, I am glad I am freed from reacting to them as though they were an instant menace.

"Words can break your bones" is a truth I have seen over and over again in marital conflicts. While perhaps more of our pathology comes from what we *observe* in our homes, some of it most assuredly comes from what we *hear*.

When mother held her little girl and said to a friend, "All men are unfaithful" or "Sex is dirty" or "I just tolerate it when he makes me get in bed," it registered! The little girl who sat on that lap or stood by that chair will be inside the adult forever. That lingering child may cause little or no harm but then again may be devastating to the adult relationship! If the imprint on the mind is highly negative, and if the inner child remains unnoticed and unsupervised, the mischief making could linger forever.

When mother speaks optimistically and positively it, too, registers. Our "computer" works with whatever is programmed into it.

The little boy, sitting by his dad on the porch or in the boat or standing out of the way while the men talk, will hear, compute, and consign his impressions to his eternal memory bank. He may hear, "Women are special and are real people too." He may hear, "Keep 'em barefoot, pregnant, and in the kitchen!" He may hear, "Take what you want and give only what you have to give to get what you want!"

He will "hear" (perceive) a lot of things, good and bad, deliberate and inadvert, but it is all stored in the little boy who will remain the constant companion of his adult. Someday that child will emerge in a controlled or an uncontrolled way to affect the quality of his marriage.

And so, many of our attitudes in marriage, and *of* marriage, were programmed into our memory bank by words or attitudes way back when. It is by being aware that this can be so, *has* to be so, that we bring greater health to our marriage.

Return of the Spoiled Brat

There are millions of illustrations of the principle under scrutiny here. I have endless case studies in my own records but might just as well tell one more on myself. All of us struggle with this principle, and the stories are not all that dissimilar.

The single biggest problem I have had in my marriage is, as I mentioned in chapter one, that I was born a spoiled brat and then suffered a relapse! I was the only son, with three sisters. I was catered to and grew up expecting everything in my home to center on me.

I had to get in touch with this particular inner child, not so much to save my marriage but in order to aid and abet its continuing maturation. Sandra and I experienced some painful times in our early marriage because of this problem, my spoiled inner child.

My first practical awareness that there was a dangerous problem came in about the seventh year of our marriage. One morning as we were traveling the two hours from our home to visit my parents in central Florida, my wife innocently encouraged me to be careful when we got to my family home. She pointed out that she had noticed I was quite a mature and adult person until I stepped into that old environment. Then I became what she tactfully referred to as a spoiled brat.

This made me so mad that I had to admit, *almost* immediately, that any accusation that would make me so angry deserved some objective scrutiny. Throughout that day and for subsequent weeks I continued to reflect on her statement, evaluate the record, be aware of evoking stimuli, and finally concluded that she was right. I did have an automatic tendency to become "little Deanie" as soon as I walked through my parents' door. I did the same thing in our home, to some degree, but was especially bad in the old environment.

Isn't it often easier to remain in the old pattern of the inner child than to develop our social personality? I have been forever glad that I began that day on the highway to get in touch with this particular dictatorial little kid within me. Getting him under control has added greater maturity to my relationship with my wife.

Not Quite Good Enough!

Joyce talked to me extensively about her problem with self-esteem in general and her feeling of never being good enough in particular. She had grown up in a good home with loving parents who gave her much and expected much from her. Many times Joyce would come home on report-card day with three A's and one B. If I had come home with three A's and one B, my parents would have thrown a party!

Not so with Joyce. Her parents would say, "That's wonderful! That's just outstanding! *But* . . . why not four A's?"

After she was married, Joyce would often sit with her husband at the evening meal and finally break the silence and the peace of the setting by saying, "I know this isn't good enough. I know you expect more from me."

He enjoyed her cooking. He didn't know what was going on, nor did she. Basically, she was saying, "Dad, please be happy with my three A's and one B. I know you never are and I can't stand the suspense any longer, so I'll say it for you."

This family became much happier when Joyce got in touch with this inner child and her subconscious transference. The problem is still not resolved. She is working at it, however, and is at least conscious of the similarity of stimuli in the two domestic settings: the home of her childhood and her present home. She is endeavoring to keep her husband separate from the expectations of her dad. Wouldn't it be helpful to your marriage to allow the person you're living with to speak and feel for themselves?

Mid-Life Crisis at Twenty-Five!

Harry's wife came to see me because, "Harry is going through the middle-age crazies." Only Harry was just twenty-five! He did have all the symptoms, however. He wanted to run and play and avoid responsibility. He wanted to wear a linen shirt open at the top to reveal the necklace nestled in his hairy chest. He wondered if he was still attractive.

Harry's wife and I met for two or three sessions. He would not come. Those who are throwing it all away while envisioning themselves as having "gotten it all together" are seldom strong enough to seek help. So, she and I visited and what emerged was revealing.

It was so simple, in fact, as to be dangerous. It's just the kind of story that prompts us to believe that all complex problems have simple answers. They do not, of course, but this one did and is reported here because again it simplistically underlines the premise of our study.

Harry had grown up in that coastal community of west Florida. He had lived on the outer edge of town when the area was all scrub pines and swampland. His favorite tree, where he and his playmates built their first NO-Girls tree house, was about the only landmark remaining from the good old days of his childhood. Everything else was paved, sprawling suburbs.

Harry drove by that tree every morning and evening going to and from work. He told Debbie that it was in the mornings and late afternoons that he experienced an almost overwhelming need to escape the requirements of marriage, child, and job.

I suggested that Debbie encourage Harry to drive to and from work by a different route—that he find an alternate route so built-up and different from "back when" that nothing could remind him of his less-complicated days. He did. The problem cleared up, to await its true time at the onset of his real mid-life crazies!

Harry's old oak tree, with its spreading branches and soothing Spanish moss, was a stimulus triggering old tapes from his memory bank. These old tapes deserve remembering and are beautiful to recall and replay. But, they are devastating when they dictate the dance of adulthood! Unchecked, they can and do disrupt marriage. They can and do create feelings, distort perspectives, and dictate terms that can be extremely disruptive to our adult relationships.

Betrayed by Unremembered Memories

Bill and his wife had been married for twenty-five years but were getting a divorce because he thought she was unfaithful. I asked Bill if he knew that for a fact. He said, "No, but I just feel it. I have felt it all these years!" They separated, but he continued to see me in an effort to explore his own contributions to the breakdown of the marriage.

At one session, after much trust had been established, Bill began painfully to explore his earliest childhood and his "perfect mother." He loved her and she loved him, and it is always painful to find fault under those circumstances.

One memorable day he finally shared with me that during his preschool years, after his father would leave for work, his mother would take him with her to visit her boyfriend.

With great pain, and probably for the first time in his life, he finally said, "She'd leave me in the living room to play while she played in the bedroom."

Neither of us spoke for a while. Bill had shared something in that moment that he had pretended all his life never existed. He simply sat there in anguish and grief. Then, he looked into my eyes with a quizzical stare and asked, "Is this why I've always hounded my wife about her unfaithfulness?"

I didn't say, "What do you think," as I am supposed to. I said, "Of course! Of course!"

Bill left my office immediately to look for his wife. When he found her, he found her remarried and happy for the first time in her adult life.

Bill had allowed his hurting, ashamed inner child to run amuck until that child had destroyed his adult happiness. When he did get in touch with that child, it was a case of too little too late.

Hugh Missildine says:

> The way we treat ourselves in adult life is critical for our mental health, happiness, and productivity. It affects everything we feel and everything we achieve or fail to achieve. If we do "what comes naturally," we tend to treat ourselves in adult life as we were treated when we were growing up. We recreate the old home atmosphere of long ago.
>
> We have a powerful built-in tendency to do this. It's almost as if a great flywheel inside keeps pulling us back to the old atmosphere. Particularly when we are tired, ill, overloaded with responsibility, or under stress *we go home*. And going home means treating ourselves as we were treated back in childhood.

It is always easier to *be* our domestic personality than to *become* our social personality!

The inner child, the pain-that-articulates-itself, our childhood pathology, is very much with us and is part and parcel of all we are or attempt to become.

The question we now need to address is: What do we do about it? How does one raise this child and control this force so that it contributes in a constructive way to our adult lives and, particularly, our marriage!

CHAPTER 4

Rearing the "Little You"

Having established the importance and difficulty of identifying or recognizing the inner child as it affects marriage, we can now concentrate on *how* the inner child is recognized and reared.

It is important to point out that this chapter concentrates on how to recognize, rear, or govern the child and not on marriage, per se. Because inner-child feedback to the adult is all-pervasive—affecting faith, health, job, self-esteem, world view, as well as marriage—any practical approach would have to concentrate on the principle of the child in general.

The inner children affecting one's marriage are reared no differently than the ones disrupting our social life, job, or faith. The rules are universally applicable and therefore the *rules* are the focus here. These are practical guidelines for persons interested in rearing the little personalities of the past who still inhabit and inhibit the adult.

1. Be Aware of the Reality and the Implications

The first guideline is fundamentally a reiteration and reaffirmation of chapter three. This basic principle must be briefly restated here, however, because it *is* a guideline and it is the *first* guideline.

We cannot deal creatively with what we will not accept as real! Without the awareness that there *are* little boys and girls still within us, we cannot function adequately in our adult world and, specifically, in our marriage.

43

One brief illustration will serve to recap this principle as well as to restate it as the first guideline.

When I was a very little kid growing up, I enjoyed sitting (only we "set") on the back porch with my dad at the end of a long day. He really enjoyed his coffee! It was not long before I began to associate coffee with being a "big man" and thus began requesting my own cup. My dad would always explain that coffee is something you can't drink until you are grown up. I accepted that, reluctantly, and waited.

Finally, when I got away to college and immediately became a "big man," I began drinking coffee regularly. I still enjoy a cup or two a day and *to this day* feel so big and so mature when I drink coffee, especially when I order a cup in public!

The scenario is not usually evident to others (thankfully) but nevertheless obvious and always the same to me. I walk into a restaurant. I sit at the counter looking cool and trying not to appear overly mature. I say to the waitress with obvious understatement, "I'd like a cup of coffee, please!" It's all I can do to keep my mouth closed and not roll my tongue around and look like a little kid who's just mastered the world.

She, in turn, gets my coffee, plops it on the counter and says, "Here it is, Mac."

I am left very much aware that she has somehow missed the response called for in the script I am personally following! I laugh about it and enjoy the inner-child play now. It is an amusing inside joke to me but no joking matter when a similar scenario emerges in marriage.

Many are the times we enter our home, bedroom, or bed and ask our husband or wife to participate in a script they have never read. We hold preconceptions of how they should act or respond to affirm our personhood or sexuality and they, simply following what we request, fail to meet our expectations. We feel hurt, misunderstood, nonaffirmed, or perhaps even devastated. This is not usually their fault. The fault, more often than not, can be found in the fact that we are not attuned to the presence and functioning of our own inner child!

This is precisely why I reiterate chapter three as the first guideline. As someone has observed, "You can only be a child once but you can be immature forever."

Or, as I have put it, we either control the inner child or the inner child controls us!

Great news! We do not always have to identify the specific child and his or her specific input. Simply being on working ground with the principle will open many valuable doors.

Guideline number ONE is: Be aware of the reality and the implications of your inner child. Nothing affects the quality and direction of your marriage more than does this concept.

2. Identify Your Danger Signals

Each of us has some pretty definite and unique danger signals which can effectively inform us that some inner child is about to take over our adult.

When we make a conscious effort to care for and maintain our marriage, we can become pretty astute at recognizing these indicators. Certain feelings or perspectives can warn us that old tapes are starting to play and if we do not want to dance to that tune, then we'd better check the music! These signals are never terribly obvious or we would have picked up on them sooner. This child, or old tape, never pulls on our nightshirt and announces his imminent arrival. He is considerate enough, however, to give some warning. It is up to us to learn to identify our own peculiar signals.

This takes some discipline and conscious tuning in to our own physical reactions in different situations. Personally, I have two distinct signals that warn me about an attempted takeover by my inner child. Sometimes these signals appear in plenty of time for me to plan my strategy. At other times they arrive with about as much warning as the report of a rifle before the striking of the bullet. My warning signals are most often a tendency toward pouting and a penchant for rushed speech.

I have learned that when I start feeling pouty, my spoiled brat of the past is trying to take over my marriage. This usually means I am getting ready to manipulate the present conflict with my wife so that it will turn in my favor. By pouting I am reinforcing that "Mommy should do what *I* want or need."

The rushed speech is basically a symptom of early-childhood insecurity. Having been raised in a home with three sisters, it is an effort to overwhelm my opposition with staccato speech. When I sense that rushing tendency, I know how to consciously put the adult in charge of the emerging child. Becoming conscious of these clear signals in my own life has greatly aided and abetted the maturation of my own marriage. I am grateful for this awareness.

What special danger signals do you have? What early-warning signs do you have that can inform you of the onset of lethal mechanisms or approaches that are going to add to your marital problems, not solve them? These, your own early-warning signals, can help you identify and control the child trying to emerge and take charge.

There are some rather classic signs. Marriage counselors dealing with this problem have a rather common list that would suggest universal applicability.

One of these early-warning signals is sleepiness. It is not uncommon to hear someone say as did a man in my office quite recently, "When my wife is mad at me, I get sleepy." As we worked on the cause of this, the pathology became clear.

When his mother would scold him as a very small boy, she either sent him to bed, or he went outside to daydream under a tree. He might even sit in a corner with his thumb in his mouth and sulk drowsily.

He could not stand conflict then or now. This was his way of checking out of the situation as best he could. Sleepiness warned him that he was getting ready to run, perhaps without even leaving the room.

Getting sleepy did not solve his marital problems. It only infuriated his wife. This, in turn, made him sleepier, which made her madder, which made him . . . Sleepiness is an often-heard symptom. Is it one of yours?

Another of the more common signs is a feeling of tightness around one's head. One man told me he had learned his inner child (not the term he used) was threatening to take over when all of a sudden he felt as though someone were tightening a steel band about his head.

We never did arrive at a clear early-childhood causal factor for this particular symptom. This could have been caused by *a* situation way back when or, more probably, a constant situation or environment in his formative years. Interestingly, he associated the same symptom with riding on an elevator, getting into a plane or anyplace where he felt boxed in or trapped. Finding *the* cause is seldom as important as simply being aware that old tapes are playing and must not be allowed to dictate the dance.

Tightening may not be brought on for you by feeling trapped but may be a symptom of anxiety over stress or conflict. It can be reaction to guilt. All of these pressures can derive from a present stressful or guilt-ridden situation. The sensation can be rooted in a similarly stressful situation in the past and triggered by something in the present.

Another often-mentioned signal is the feeling of stupidity. Many of us are getting ready to experience inner-child takeover when our marriage partner's words or actions make us feel that we are stupid, even when they were not meant in that manner.

In the case of one young lady, certain voice tones her husband occasionally used *reminded* her of how her dad talked to her when giving her his favorite speech about "Why wasn't she as good a student as her sister." She felt stupid then and continues to have the same feelings when her husband inadvertently and unknowingly uses the same voice inflection. *What* he said did not warrant such feelings. She is simply listening to tapes activated from way back when. Now she is in the process of learning that the feeling of being stupid just may be an early-warning symptom. This helps to keep her living in the present.

There are other common early danger signals that may spare your marriage added pressure from the past: an impending sense of fear, a feeling of being overwhelmed, a debilitating sense of jealousy. You may feel a sudden sensation of just being wiped out or too tired to go on. There may be other feelings that are peculiarly unique to your past life and present world. Learn to recognize them.

These signals may vary somewhat from person to person, but most are pretty common and can be enormously serviceable. They can serve to inform us that something from back then is getting ready to disrupt, or *further* disrupt, something in our marriage *now*.

Good marriages are not void of conflict. Friction is inevitable in closeness. Good marriages make creative use of conflict. One way of doing this is by learning how to identify the early-warning signals of the impending inner child. This second guideline, recognizing your danger signals, can be of great help in your effort to care for and maintain a good marriage.

3. Love and Nourish That Hurting or Neglected Child

The healthy and creative little children within us do not need a lot of specific attention. Their contribution to the success of our marriage is usually quite spontaneous and positive. These positive and vibrant children need but sporadic attention and general nurture.

It is our child who is troubled and denied who will cause so much mischief. This is the one we need to recognize as well as afford systematic love and specific nourishment as we move toward control and maturation. After all, most children anywhere who are disruptive tend to be so not because they are so bad, but because they are so neglected. They want love and attention and will persist in being holy terrors until someone gives them attention: punishment if need be, but love if possible. This is true of children within our family who disrupt our home as well as children within ourselves who destroy our marriage.

This sensible and creative approach is not our natural inclination, especially as it relates to the children within us. Our natural instinct seems to be one of neglect or more often suppression. We seem to prefer the misguided notion that a troublesome child unacknowledged somehow ceases to exist. A brat kept bottled up ceases to function!

Quite the opposite is true! An inner child who is negative and is neglected, especially through suppression, just grows bigger and meaner and more disruptive. It's like ignoring a lump in the body until it becomes a malignant threat to life. It's like overlooking a small problem in marriage until it becomes an undeniable threat to the marriage.

Little children within us who are starved for attention will simply fester and grow until they cannot be ignored! When they grow big enough, they will break through the lids and chains placed over and about them and come crashing into our adult world with a strength and size that may prove unmanageable. Historically, or chronologically, this undeniable and unrestrainable state is usually reached when the adult reaches mid-life.

Just the other day Barbara (not her real name) came to my office in tears. She said, "My husband is going through the mid-life crazies! He is now doing absolutely everything he has always loathed in others. He has, from day one of our marriage, been critical of immature, rebellious men who cheat on their wives. Now that's exactly what *he's* doing! What on earth is going on?"

I was glad she asked! Being ordained and infallible in all things, I certainly knew! I had seen it a thousand times and willingly shared my perceptions with her.

Her husband, like a lot of husbands and wives, had gone through perhaps thirty-five years of life not only neglecting a bruised and battered little person within but suppressing its existence.

As we suppress this little child, we often find that we form a great dislike for other people who have the same traits that we are suppressing. We dislike noisy or rebellious people, negative or unfaithful people. It can be any overt type of activity that is a clear manifestation of our suppressed child.

We may be able to deny our own inclinations in this direction for many years. But all the time, this little child is a time bomb waiting to go off. This festering, growing, suppressed being within finally reaches overwhelming size around mid-life and bursts on the scene to demand a hearing. We are overwhelmed and find ourselves becoming what we have always loathed.

The brat has got to be let out of the bottle if he is to be recognized and nourished to maturity.

For the sake of our marriage we must give our neglected inner children understanding and healthy attention. This healthy attention and nourishment to which I have regularly alluded is achieved by giving *that* child what every child needs and craves, full acceptance as a real person! He needs to be talked to, instructed, and otherwise helped in the maturation process. He needs the security of knowing that the adult is in ultimate control and that the child, though he may attempt to erupt onto the scene, will be allowed to go just so far.

Rule number three is: If our lingering child can play such a positive and negative part in our adult marriage, then we must love and nourish that presence. This presence has either joy to give or misery to foster. The responsibility for deciding which of these will be predominant rests on our sensitivity and sensibility as the adult. Neglect and denial must be replaced with awareness and nourishment.

4. Be Aware That Not All Children Are Easy to Raise

There are, of course, some children in our homes and within our-selves who *are* easy to raise. They are healthy, loving, pliable, and "no trouble at all." Others, however, do not submit easily to adult control. Not only are they bruised or hurt to begin with—if ne-glected for thirty-five years, they become raging habits. And, raging habits are not easily broken! Compounding this problem is that we do not want to break our child, only his negative control over our marriage. We do not want to kill that energy but learn to harness and direct it.

This difficulty of rearing some children goes back to a point I raised earlier. Do not perceive what I am saying as a quick, easy so-lution to severe personal or marital problems. Just because you know that there is a disruptive little child within you does not mean all is well! Not many of our children will be handled quickly or without consistent effort on our part.

In many cases the inner child will not make an easy treaty with the adult. Old and bad habits are not that easily broken. That child can treat you or your marriage viciously! He or she can be irra-tional, throw temper tantrums, and generally cause all-out guerrilla warfare between you and yourself or you and your mate. He will assume a stance of submission and compliance only to spring into action when your guard is dropped. He can embrace you with a vi-cious grip causing destructive conflict at the very point when your marriage most needs tolerance and communication.

Be prepared to enter this difficult civil war with all-out commit-ment. Let your specific goal be that of becoming the benevolent dictator when there can be no treaty. Better you rule your inner child if you cannot rear him, than allow him to rule and ruin your marriage!

In this all-outness be ready to use every tool at your disposal. Lecture the child, love the child, be understanding, be rough. Kid with him or stand on his neck, but be in charge!

Often, when some early-warning signals inform me that one of my little ones is on the way, I will tease him or otherwise confront him with humor. With one or two, I've already learned I can't whip or outwit them, so I make fun of them. I say, "There you are you little rascal! Come out on the porch and let's talk about what you are getting ready to do to my marriage." I try to talk, tease, or kid with him.

We must! We dialogue or we duel! If we can learn to dialogue, then our marriage has a chance to sail. If we persist in dueling, then our marriage most probably will suffer. If we cannot talk with him, then we must remember that the angry, dueling child is, and probably will always be, tough to rear. We must stay in charge on any account.

Be as tough as you have to. Some children are not easily reared. Be like the Englishman visiting this country for the first time. When asked to comment on the American home he said, "The greatest need of the American home is that the children be taught that 'No!' is a complete sentence!"

You may have to be like the child expert who passed a little fella on a motorized horse in front of a department store. His mother could not coax him off the horsie with all her understanding and applied psychology. Recognizing the famous expert, she enlisted his help.

He walked over to the little boy and whispered into his ear. The little boy immediately got off the horse and returned meekly to his mother. The mother was impressed and insisted on knowing what wonderful insights the psychologist had shared with her son to get him to behave so promptly.

The doctor replied, "I said to him, 'Little boy, if you don't get down off that horse this instant and return to your mother, I'll break your skinny little arm!' "

You may have to do just that with *some* of your inner children. I know I do! I have an inner child or three I suspect I shall never fully bring to maturity and creativity. They may never be harnessed or totally conquered, and détente is out of the question. As mentioned before, one problem is the spoiled brat evoked by not getting my way. The other is my tendency to rush my speech when I think no one is listening. I have more years to bring these to maturity, but I just may spend the rest of my life simply holding a gun to their head! If I cannot make them a creative force in my life, at least I can be tough enough to prevent them from being a periodic disruptive force within my marriage.

Be aware that your child who disrupts your personality or your marriage is not always easily brought to creative maturity. Love and nourish the ones you can and hold a stick over the others. Teach them that "No!" is a complete sentence. Say to your child, "No! you cannot control this situation. You cannot have your way this time!"

5. Look for New Role Models

So many of our inner-child conflicts and many of our adult problem areas come from our initial role models. These may have been family members, friends, or images given us by society. We saw, perceived, and assimilated approaches to marriage difficulties, problems of the world, and society. Now we need to see how it can be done differently. Some of these early models need replacing. There are other more suitable and healthy approaches. Finding people who can expose us to new models is of practical consequence. It is easier to nurture and rear some inner child if we can *see* how the child should act.

Selecting new role models, people who act differently in and about marriage than did our parents, has obvious limitations. You can't, for instance, go home with someone and watch them make love just because this is the problem you are having and for which you need a new model. That would be somewhat unacceptable!

You could, however, observe those about you at church, in the shopping mall, at the office, who do show you how to be freer in sharing and showing affection. Most people who have trouble in bed also have trouble in the head at the point of being vulnerable, spontaneous, and demonstrative.

This is usually a "like father like son, like mother like daughter" situation. We bring behavior patterns from these early models, in stored tapes, to our adult relationship. The tapes are then played over and over until we choose to play them differently or find new models to show us how. Movie and TV models help very little because we constantly remind ourselves (and should!) that they are not real people and are "Hollywoodized."

Not so with real, healthy, sensible couples about you. Find someone who is good at what you need to be better at and secretly let them teach you how.

If your trouble is guarded spontaneity, find someone who is vivacious and gregarious in a healthy way. If your problem is being too unguarded and spontaneous, allow some healthy peer to show you how to be less of an extrovert. If you have trouble communicating with your wife or husband, then learn from someone who can show you how it is done. All this new data will carry over to the bedroom or any intimate area where the real you must function.

One of the early problems my wife and I had in our marriage was my inability to enjoy a group situation. This tended to make us both ill at ease in social interactions. My wife enjoys being with others and wanted both of us to enjoy such occasions. I was handicapped, however! I lived in a very small town and did no traveling until I went away to college; so there was not much chance for any social orientation. I liked people and enjoyed being in a group, but I simply did not know how to act. My inner child kept me uncomfortable even as an adult.

I needed a new role model so that I could teach this child what he had not learned, or perhaps needed to relearn, from a rather limited social exposure.

I frequently found myself around a man from my office who was an excellent role model for this troublesome inner child of mine. He was the son of a diplomat and had traveled extensively. He was, perhaps more importantly, a genuinely caring and obviously healthy, well-adjusted person. I watched *how* he interacted with people. I especially watched my friend, when all the couples from the office were at social functions, as he and his wife interacted with others. While I did not make an A on the course, he taught me a great deal. I continue to work on this deficiency in my own marriage and can do so because I have observed others.

After you have become aware of the principle of the inner child, and after you have identified a child or so who need to mature, you can help yourself by watching someone who knows how to do whatever it is you need to do better!

6. Get Outside the Conflict

The sixth rule is one of the simplest guidelines on the list and one I have personally found to be most practical and beneficial. Get outside the conflict! *Conflict* is not to be translated as "the marriage." The word *conflict* refers here to the conflict being caused *in* the marriage by an inner child butting heads with the adult. That is conflict!

To get outside the conflict, therefore, means to find a way to be more objective about how to handle that troublesome child about to disrupt our marriage.

The child may be low self-esteem that places your partner in the bind of having to provide you with an unrealistic quantity of affirmation. It may be a presence from long ago when Dad was unfaithful to Mom, or vice versa, that causes you today to be uncommonly jealous. Your inner child may be affecting your present marriage in many ways; but that child is so subjectively a part of your life that you cannot view him constructively without some practical tool.

Ask yourself, then, what advice would I give a close friend who was in creative struggle with this (my) specific inner child? Most of us can rather easily tell someone else how to handle a problem better than we can handle our own problems. Decide what you would tell your friend about that problem and then go do it yourself. Follow your advice to them! That's what is meant by getting outside the conflict. Find a way to gain some degree of objectivity over the situation so you will know what to do or say to that specific child currently disrupting your marriage.

Gain objectivity by getting outside the conflict and then act on that good advice.

7. Practice Separation Therapy

Separation therapy is the developed skill of knowing when our child is in charge of our adult. It is going a step beyond the sixth guideline of getting outside the conflict, to working consistently at following up on objectivity. It is the learned and *practiced* capacity of maintaining adult control over the child.

It is the old adage that practice makes perfect and is certainly the concluding guideline in rearing the child of the past. Because so many of these children are tyrants or simply unwilling to establish an easy treaty with the adult, keeping on keeping on is imperative. Practice does make for the possibility of perfect control.

You may be like the man who came to my office recently in deep distress over his inability to control a specific inner child in his life. He knew who and what the child was! He had already discovered that there was a presence within him, a remnant of his early child-hood, and he had it labeled but not bridled. His father was an afflu-ent and overworked doctor. He was generous and lavished everything on his family except quality time.

Our young man, in growing up, had set as his goal a much more leisurely life-style. He also wanted to continue the same generosity exhibited by his father. That was rather a self-defeating goal to begin with. You can't have enough money to spread all those good things around by doing little to get that money. This was, neverthe-less, his goal.

By the time I had seen him for the umpteenth time, he had al-ready discovered this disruptive model he had established for him-self. He had also seen rather clearly how it was affecting his marriage. In practical application, for instance, he had pursued a much less demanding and proportionately less remunerating career but still wanted his wife to spend lavishly. She did and he stayed angry about the financial bind he constantly encouraged through his old pathology.

He saw that the problem was a conflicting and self-defeating goal. He was painfully aware of the child within as well as his in-ability to keep that child separated from his adult. He would tell me in great anguish, "I know the child is there. I ask him to stop dis-rupting my marriage, but he will not!" I would always answer, "He hasn't *yet!*"

Keep practicing! Keep on keeping on until practice provides the avenue to possibility. Be relentless in demanding that the child either mature or submit willingly, or unwillingly, to adult control.

I have some inner children (and so do you) that affect my mar-riage dearly and drastically. I must consciously *practice* develop-ment or control as the case may require.

Keeping the child actively helping our marriage or from dis-rupting our marriage is not something learned quickly and easily. It is definitely not done once and for all. A conscious, consistent effort must be made if one is to be a vigorous practitioner of separating and controlling all the little voices within. Keep practicing until you can keep the voice of the child separated from the reality of the adult.

The inner child is a real presence and potential power, for good or bad, in one's marriage. Probably nothing else affects our adult relationships as strongly as do these old tapes, these inner children of the past. They must be identified and reared. The way this is done is basically the same way one would rear any child, the child of our home, the child affecting our job, the child disrupting our faith, or the child aggravating our marriage. In these basic guidelines I have attempted to state some of the more important rules in rearing a child *whatever* or *wherever* they may be found. They are sound principles and important handles on getting the job done.

The inner-child principle and these guidelines for implementing it are not intended to imply that *all* marriage problems stem from our early childhood. This chapter (and the preceding one) is a simple statement that *many* of our struggles and disruptions are so centered. The problems we do have in our marriage that are rooted in our earlier years can best be dealt with through understanding something of the what and the how of the inner-child principle. These children of the past are there and they do cause *many* of our adult problems.

"We never grow up, so it seems. We keep in our hearts all our dreams and in a corner we find, tucked away, the child we all were yesterday." That child, your child, needs to be reared by an adult, your adult!

CHAPTER 5

Scratching Where It Itches: External Factors

In the course of *any* marriage there will be periods of discomfort, distraction, and despair. I shall refer to this general and predictable condition as "itching." One of the tricks to be learned in the care and maintenance of a good marriage is how to scratch where it itches.

That itching is inevitable is not only predictable but a logical assumption. Whenever two people are close, there will be friction. Whenever two people begin a life together, there is yet a lifetime of growth and maturity before them. Growth and maturity are costly and often uncomfortable. Whenever two people start the process of establishing a solid home, they will inevitably discover the old truth: everyone is hard to live with! In a good marriage our partner will give us enough to make it worthwhile, but there will be real discomfort, severe itching. Every married couple has to learn how to deal with the discomfort. Just don't break and run! Funny thing about itching in your marriage, you can't outrun it. Itching is part of the normal process of living closely and maturing together in marriage.

This phenomenon of itching, and the accompanying need to deal with it directly and realistically, will be explored in this chapter and the next. There are *external* and *internal* causes of marital discomfort. In this chapter we shall look at the two most common *external* causes of marital discomfort. Chapter six will deal with the three most common *internal* causes.

Perhaps the best way to get at the essence of both of these chapters is to begin with what many call "The Seven Year Itch Syndrome."

The idea that chief periods of discomfort come at somewhat predictable stages is a theory held, with different descriptions and nomenclatures, by many marriage counselors. It derives from the observation that our most severe periods of marital adjustment (itch) *seem* to appear at seven-year increments. This theory, or observation, is extremely unscientific! However, it is easily documented. No one can prove it, but it is equally difficult to deny.

For instance, how many times have you heard someone say, "They've been married twenty-one years and are getting a divorce! Can you believe that?" How often have we heard, "I just hate to throw away fourteen good years"? How many times has she said to him, "It's only been seven years! Let's give it more time"? And, we are all fully conversant with the phrase "The Seven Year Itch."

As a marriage counselor I am no longer surprised, because the syndrome is so constant! In fact, after hearing the introductory scenario of a marriage in trouble, I will often ask if they have been married seven years, fourteen, or twenty-one. The answer almost inevitably is one of these, or twenty-eight, give or take a year either way. The theory of "The Seven Year Incremental Syndrome" is extremely unscientific and unbelievably persistent.

Mentioning this observation is somewhat dangerous because of its potential for negative suggestion. Some sweet, trusting soul will say, "Oh my! We've been so happy up till now. I guess next year is the year we pay our dues!" They plan for it, prepare for it, and usually are not disappointed.

On the other hand it does not need to be either programmed or an unexpected problem. Most marriages will face some major incremental adjustment periods, and it's better to be forewarned than ambushed! Many couples are truly helped in their adjustment when they discover the universality of their predicament. They no longer feel isolated and unique. When we perceive ourselves as involved in normal, predictable situations, we are much more apt to handle the situation in a creative way.

Marriage counselors, clinical psychologists, and psychiatrists will smile knowingly, and perhaps even with some degree of self-consciousness, when this theory is mentioned. I think this is not because the theory fails the test of universality but because no one is really sure of the cause.

Some counselors suggest, for instance, that the syndrome is caused by psychological factors—that our body cells change totally every seven years and this may trigger subtle and telling emotional waves.

Others offer the theory of natural fatigue. The older anything gets the more it is subject to normal and natural fatigue. A marriage, like the body, or an automobile, or home appliance wears down and becomes more prone to stress with time and travel.

Still others who search for the causal factor of the syndrome speak of "natural confluences." Carl Jung, the renowned pioneer in psychiatry, used the term *synchronicity*. Natural confluence, or synchronicity, implies that given enough time things will get together like two rivers ultimately meeting to form one, or two events synchronizing to appear as a planned event.

For instance, by the seventh year of an average marriage, romantic love has been somewhat replaced by realistic and maturing love. By the fourteenth year of that marriage the children are entering their most difficult and exasperating years—the teens. Disruptive thirteen-year-olds going on twenty-five can put enormous pressure on a marriage. By the twenty-first year of the average marriage the empty-nest syndrome has struck. In some cases, the couple is hoping it will strike! By then, the mind is still willing but the flesh is weaker. Also, the jobs of one or both of the marriage partners may not have turned out to be the panacea for which they had hoped. Then, in due time and due course a disease called middle-age crazies also begins to run rampant. Given enough time and space, things will just flow together and yet appear programmed or designed. This is the theory of synchronicity, or natural confluence.

No one is sure which theory accurately pinpoints the cause of the syndrome. Perhaps all these factors, and more, conspire to cause the seven-year itch. What we are sure about is that there will be periodic itching. There will be regular and common periods of discomfort throughout the daily life of two people who stand close to each other. But, there also will be very strong periods of *unusual* discomfort and these can be expected, for whatever reason, every half-dozen or so years.

We must be careful that we do not become preoccupied with the

symptom and ignore the cause. Cause is everything! You don't have
a problem because you want to break up your marriage. You want
to break up your marriage because you have a problem, and it is the
cause we seek out! You don't have a problem because you itch. You
itch because you have a problem! We must ignore the symptom and
go for the cause.

Not the painful, distracting symptoms, but the *cause* of itching in
any good marriage is the focus of this chapter and the next. Let's
look first at the external factor of *normality*.

What Is Normal?

Most of us would not recognize normal if it walked in and bit us
on the foot! We have simply grown accustomed to the world we live
in. It is known in some circles as the real world. In this so-called real
world we have grown so accustomed to abnormal that normal
seems out of place if, in fact, it is even recognizable.

Our orientation and acclimation can be compared with that of a
little child lying on his bed on his back with his head dangling over
the edge of the mattress. If he lies in that position long enough,
looks at the room upside down long enough, the room begins to
look right-side up. Then he suddenly sits up and finds that what was
once right-side up now appears to be upside down. So it is that our
world of tinsel, quick fix, substitution, and instant everything seems
normal while normalities of the past seem strangely out of place.

We find ourselves confused, disoriented, and we can't quite put
our finger on the problem. Not only are we confused by the subtleness of it all but, as men have always done, we adjust. We do this to
preserve our sanity. We seek to stabilize our world by redefining
normality.

We are like the San Francisco architect I heard about who hated
an old Victorian mansion he had to pass going to work each day.
After several years of agony over confronting this particular aesthetic aberration, he bought the old house, moved in, got used to it,
and never saw the ugly old house again. Such has been our adjustment! We have bought it, moved in, and the ugly abnormalities of
the past now seem quite normal.

This problem is further complicated by the fact that normality
does change! What is normal (defining *normal* as that which is tra-

ditional, healthy, and stabilizing to a society) can pass through legitimate metamorphosis.

For instance, I performed a wedding at Trinity Church a few months ago that still intrigues me. I live in a community that boasts of two fine colleges. They have a combined enrollment of about 45,000 students. In a community of this nature, as in the nation generally, the practice of abortion is accepted by many. The prevailing attitude seems to be, if you have a problem kill it!

A specific young couple I married did not share this particular mentality. They came to me and informed me that she was pregnant. They loved each other and wanted to do the responsible thing. They had decided to be married and have their child.

The wedding was one of the most beautiful I have ever seen. I felt especially honored to be part of such a commitment. All the bride's sorority sisters came, the groom's fraternity brothers turned out en masse. Everyone knew the bride was pregnant but everyone cried, hugged, smiled, and was glad. It was the abnormal thing become normal!

I could not help remembering that twenty-five years ago when I performed my first wedding, all this would have been a scandal. Today it not only *seemed* right, but compared to widely accepted alternatives, it *was* the right thing given the circumstances.

So in establishing the idea of what is normal in marriage, we face the further complication that normal can change and has changed in certain cases.

Our perception of what is normal has great impact on the care and maintenance of our marriage. If we know what is normal, or what has become healthy-normal in a given situation, then we work and react from a more stable foundation. We are thus enabled more properly to evaluate whether certain feelings are okay, and therefore should not be suppressed. We have a much better handle on situations or feelings and do not slip into panic and overreaction. If we know that it is normal to feel down, discouraged, out of love, and so forth, we have then captured a great asset for our goal of care and maintenance of a good marriage. There are always times in a good marriage when we must be able to say, "This feeling is normal. Hang tough and see it through!"

A lady who had been married about thirteen and one-half years came to my office for an appointment. She began her story with a look that could only be described as fear bordering on panic. She said, "All of a sudden I have come to realize that I no longer like my husband." What I really wanted to say in response was, "I know your husband and nobody likes your husband! Don't worry about it. It's no big deal!" But that wasn't the point. The point was that she had liked him and wanted to continue to like him. Now, all of a sudden, she was riddled with anxiety over the thought that she was losing what had been important to her life.

Once she controlled her panic and gave the situation a little time, she realized this was not the case at all. She was not losing her love for her husband. She was simply passing through a *normal* period generated perhaps by growth, frustration, too much closeness, or any number of things that accompany even good marriages. Being unable to recognize the normality of this situation, she had perceived the situation as abnormal. She had blown it all out of proportion, making it difficult to deal with or to understand or to ignore.

Every good marriage has times just like those that this lady was experiencing. Every close and loving couple have moments or days when they really don't like each other. That's normal! We simply must learn to recognize what are *normal* feelings and frustrations.

One of the great lessons I learned about normality, growth, and feelings was taught to me by my high school typing teacher. This lesson has helped me in my job, my marriage, my faith, in everything where my perception of normal is important to further growth.

This important lesson came during my junior year in high school, but I must begin the story a little further back. I was a poor student throughout my public school life. I had failed the third grade, was subsequently passed from grade to grade (to move me along), and had survived for the most part on a diet of C's and D's. In fact, I made the first A of my life in my first quarter in college!

One day, in my junior year, I felt a small inspiration. That's not unusual. It is just as normal for a certified loser to have occasional feelings of adequacy as it is for those who've got it together to have normal periods of being down.

I suddenly realized that if I could ignore what most of my teachers were telling me about myself and apply myself, I could excel!

I immediately chose typing as my test course and set my goal to be the best typist in my class. I worked at that goal and, lo and behold, I began to excel! I began to look forward to typing class and worked even harder. I particularly enjoyed the speed tests. I loved sailing around the keyboard while other students were still hunting and pecking. Never mind the mistakes, the sound was great!

The inevitable day came, however, when I encountered total frustration in my new skill. That day, and the subsequent day or so, resulted in an insight and a principle of life that has helped me innumerable times since.

I came to class that fateful day with no apparent consciousness that anything was amiss. I felt good and was just as interested as ever in making this commitment work. The teacher announced a speed drill. I was ready! She started the clock and I dove into the keyboard.

To my surprise and chagrin I was totally uncoordinated. I not only missed key after key but got my fingers stuck between keys. I missed the carriage return by a mile! I said nothing but struggled on in frustration. The next day the same thing occurred, and the next, and the next. On the fourth day I came to class determined to end this madness once and for all. We began with a speed drill, and I launched into the very same spastic behavior.

To this day, thirty years later, I remember well what happened next. I counted almost to ten, picked my big L.C. Smith typewriter up with both hands, and slammed it on my desk. This attracted the teacher's attention. She came over to where I was seated and said with admirable control, "What's your problem?" When I explained my frustrating problem to her, she surprised me by telling me she had been expecting precisely that for several weeks!

I was not a person of faith at that time, nor was I married, nor was I a student worthy of the name. But the way she explained my typing predicament has repeatedly saved my faith, marriage, and *all growing* areas of my life!

She helped me see that in all learning experiences, which would include any area where growth was mandatory, one's body or mind will simply select a stopping point. This stopping point is necessary for rest and *assimilation.* We need periods like that to solidify our gains and to prepare to continue new growth. It is a normal and healthy plateau that in the case of my typing, according to my teacher, "gave my fingers a period of rest so the rest of my body could catch up." She said, "If you will accept this period without threat or panic, it will serve its purpose and you will go back to enjoying and growing in your work."

That was the day I learned that all growing experiences have built-in plateaus for rest and assimilation, and that they are normal, imperative, and healthy.

At that time I began to see what I have clearly observed these subsequent years. A growing, dynamic marriage (like an exciting faith, meaningful job, or enjoyable leisure pursuit) experiences regular periods of normal frustration, boredom, or anxiety. A good, growing marriage has predictable periods of downness and out-of-loveness, and these are not only predictable but normal. We need to recognize this normality. We need to relax in these periods, accept them as healthy and necessary, and not be threatened or thrown into panic. They will serve their purpose, and eventually the enjoyment and growth of a good marriage will return.

A visitor to my office the other day helped me understand further this need to treat normal as normal and not to fight it. He was a World War II veteran, a marine pilot who had flown fighters in the Pacific theater.

We began discussing the various aircrafts of that day. Among other planes, I mentioned my interest in the old Bell Air-Cobra, the P-39. He remarked that he had flown that plane and that it was remarkable to recall. He pointed out that the engine of the P-39 was located about a third of the way back in the fuselage. In fact, the pilot virtually sat over the motor. A long drive shaft led to the front of the plane where the propeller flung the craft through the skies.

My friend mentioned that the unusual thing about flying this particular fighter was its strange center of gravity resulting from its unique engine mount. He explained, "When you took that ship into a steep dive and exceeded a certain speed, the plane went out of control and spun wildly in its down spiral. The uninitiated pilot would fight the stick and usually fly the plane right into the sea. Experience taught us to reduce air speed, keep your hands off the stick, allow the plane to slow down, and it would correct itself." He pointed out, "The P-39 didn't like the gyration any more than you did. If you gave it a chance and didn't fight the controls, the plane would stabilize itself."

This is why it is so important that we learn what normality is in our marriage—that we learn that in all growing, exciting involvements like marriage, there are predictable and useful interludes that allow and foster assimilation and solidification. There are plateaus that force us to slow down and keep it all together. To fight these normal periods, to panic, to think for a moment it isn't normal and that with some other partner it would be different is both destructive and counterproductive. If you have a good marriage and it is a growing marriage, you will experience plateaus where you can, if used wisely, rest from the climb. Accept the rest so you can climb again!

Programmed Subconscious

The second big external factor in learning to scratch where it itches is our *programmed subconscious.* You may read technical material referring to this same external factor as *subliminal stimuli.* Programmed subconscious, or the process of subliminal stimuli, is the precise reason we do not tend to recognize normal happenings within us and about us. Put very simply, this process is the brainwashing technique whereby a person, or society, is made to think a certain way without being aware of the process. It is stimuli bombarding our subconscious minds into submission. We are so constantly taught and shown that normal is abnormal and abnormal is normal that we rather easily assimilate such distortion into our own world view.

One simple illustration of this process was demonstrated some years ago by a company that manufactures small cigars. When the surgeon general's report first came out on the direct correlation between smoking and cancer, this cigar company decided the time was right to advocate their brand. Since cigars had escaped some of the incriminating evidence, now was their chance.

The key, evidently, was to expand the market among the female portion of the populace. Their approach was to have an attractive woman sitting in a posh restaurant holding the small cigar in her lovely gloved hand.

She did not have the cigar in her mouth, however. This was not only because having it in her mouth was against FCC rules but, more importantly, because the public was not ready *yet* to accept their pretty young things sitting in posh restaurants with stogies sticking out of their faces. Consequently, the lady sat at a table adjacent to a mirror, held the cigar up to her face, and admired the eloquence of it all.

Unknown to the casual viewer the camera angle subtly shifts so that the viewer is now observing the woman from the direction of the adjacent mirror! While the cigar is obviously an inch from her face, the predominant camera angle causes the cigar to appear to be in her mouth.

This advertisement was soon followed by one in which Mr. Average Man on the street was asked if he would consider offering a lady one of these small cigars. This procedure was repeated for several weeks. Finally there was a scene in which Mr. Average Man responded, as he had been subtly programmed to respond, by saying, "Certainly, I think it would be fine for a gentleman to offer a lady a cigar!"

All the while, this same Mr. Average Man likes to run around our society bragging, "Nobody tells me what to think! I think what I want to think!" Thus he is entrapped by the process of old-fashioned brainwashing.

The great missionary and crusader against illiteracy, Dr. Frank Laubach, put the whole thing in this perspective: "Whatever a person reads from twenty to thirty times, he begins to believe as reality."

This becomes a real problem in our marriage. We must deal with what we are being led to absorb from movies, television, magazines, and what Margaret Mead once called "the conspiracy on the home." She points out that this subconscious factor is comprised of the tons of books, films, and talk shows that constantly portray bad marriages. Sadly, she commented, it is often the people with bad marriages who write the plays, produce the movies, and write the books that teach and instill our values or lack of values. These people with an ax to grind concerning the institution of marriage seek catharsis by dumping on the public, while those with good marriages stay home and enjoy them.

It is not information that so disrupts our marriage as much as it is misinformation constantly projected and bought unknowingly by our perception of events about us. It is the pragmatic, proliferated nonsense that permeates our homes and psyches via our various mass media that not only distorts our perceptions of normality but logically spills over into our marriage to cause unnecessary stress and discomfort.

Examples of this constant brainwashing are numerous. I see many people, for instance, who have been informed and convinced that divorce is freedom and the beginning of the end of their problems. I always hurt with them as they discover that very few marriages are as bad as the divorce that is supposed to correct them!

Many, caught up in a society geared for profit at all expense, are like the lady who once said to me, "I've watched soap operas until all I could think of was having an affair. After getting used to the idea and finding such conduct rather acceptable, I had an affair and now I am absolutely devastated. It didn't work out the way it was supposed to!"

It is perhaps this brainwashing by so-called soft-core pornography that is most devastating to our perspectives concerning marriage. Hard-core pornography is usually so preposterous or absurd that it is rather easily dismissed by our mind. But the soft or soft-soft variety, as in soap operas, is having a not-so-subtle, but heavily subconscious, effect on sexuality in marriage. Couples are being repeatedly "informed" that sex, if you're a real man or real woman, is always thrilling and dramatic. This process of subliminal stimuli tends to inhibit being one's self and encourages competing in passion and performance with the actor. The process certainly makes normal plateaus seem threatening and abnormal.

Also, marriages are coming to know more cruelties because cruelty is programmed into much of today's media. We are not only shown so much violence but are introduced to "copy cat" possibilities. We are also led to believe that, in some instances, violence will "turn us on."

Much of today's subliminal stimuli encourages escape, selfishness, and neglect of responsibility. What we read, see, or perceive from twenty to thirty times, we begin to perceive as reality. What we are seeing at every turn, hundreds and hundreds of times each week, is turning us into a society hard pressed to keep up with healthy normality. This is a direct consequence of the process of visual impact that secretly programs the mind—subliminal stimuli.

If we are to properly care for and maintain our good marriage, we must learn to scratch where it itches. The two primary and interrelated external factors that must receive specific attention are: (1) the discomfort caused by not knowing with certainty what is normal and what is abnormal and (2) determining who is telling us what to think and what they are telling us to think. Scratch *there* and you will be doing your marriage a great service!

CHAPTER 6

Scratching Where It Itches: Internal Factors

Just as there are predominant external factors that cause irritants in the marriage, there are also internal factors that cause just as much discomfort. The principal ones are (1) fatigue, (2) sameness, and (3) menopause. All factors, both external and internal, are not unique to good marriages. They are to be found wherever two people seek to build a mature, growing relationship.

These factors do tend, however, to be more noticeable in a good marriage than they do when the relationship is bad. It is the same principle, for instance, as when the man with advanced bone cancer shows little concern with an ingrown toenail. The man who has never had much more than an ingrown toenail, however, considers his affliction catastrophic, because his overall health is basically good.

Thus, these normal irritants tend to stand out more in healthy marriages because they are often the major problems in the relationship. We give them much more attention and credibility than they deserve.

One of the best ways to eliminate not their presence but their *rule* in our lives is to know more about them. By examining the three most prevalent internal factors we can better control the discomfort they cause.

Too Pooped to Pop!

No athlete can get in shape *enough* that he or she can avoid arriving at an occasional state of virtually unbearable fatigue. These normal, predictable junctures are inevitably accompanied by an equally natural inclination to quit, run, or hide. As Vince Lombardi once observed, "Fatigue makes cowards of us all."

This same rule and reality is true of great jobs, a marvelous faith, the way we feel about ourselves, and the way we feel about our marriage. There is no way we can be conditioned enough or in love enough that we will not have periods when we gasp for air and pray for the final whistle.

There is no job so rewarding or so good but that we will experience times when we are as tired of it as we are inspired and motivated by it! Faith is something that can be and should be beautiful, real, and personal. There is no faith, however, especially if one is growing and moving but that one must experience such times as Paul did when he said, "I despair unto death." No matter how high our self-esteem may be, or how healthy and good our marriage may be, there will still be times of painful downness, and we might as well plan for them and thus recognize them when they arise. These, in fact, seem to be some of our best contact points for gaining perspective and reality. No marriage, no matter how good, if it is growing and dynamic, can hope to survive without points of simple, normal fatigue.

I marvel that the majority of couples handle this factor as admirably as they do. It is awesome and often overwhelming to awaken one day and discover that you are tired of your love and oppressed by your new sense of burden. Such an awakening can be most threatening, even though normal and temporary, and yet most couples seem to take it pretty much in stride. Most seem to be aware, on one level or another, that "this too shall pass." They seem to know that occasional fatigue is normal and predictable. They scratch that irritant and go on with life!

Fatigue, of course, has dimensions far beyond this expression. It enters the marriage through the work borne by the husband, and now just about as often by the wife. They both keep long, exhausting hours. Sometimes one or the other is holding down yet another job "in their free time."

Fatigue enters the picture through the advent of children. Bills pile up. Jobs are threatened. Countless other things heap exhaustion and pressure on already-frayed nerves and limited time. There is little time or energy left for sex, communication, or the simple enjoyments of life together.

Working at the personal adjustments of marriage requires a great deal of energy. Combine this with the exhausting pressures all about us and one does marvel that so many handle the problem so well. Fatigue is a fact of life, an internal fact of life, in any marriage.

This problem is further complicated by the subliminal stimuli that constantly inform us that Mr. Right/Miss Right is the key to eliminating all problems. "If I can just find the right mate . . ." The normality of fatigue escapes us! We chase about everywhere but inside ourselves.

Fatigue is always associated with commitment. We simply cannot be in shape enough, in love enough, or even committed enough to prevent normal fatigue. Anything that is dynamic has predictable and necessary points of weariness. We need to rest and rally, not run or retreat!

To put it another way, we need to be reminded not only of the normality of this internal causal factor but that patience and tenacity are everything. People who simply will not quit are those who not only enjoy life more but who also realize more of the beautiful fruits of life. As the minister Sam Jones once said, "The longer I live the more convinced I become that the difference between people: the great and the small, the rich and the poor, the noble or ignoble, is a goal once set and then victory or death!" Jones once defined optimism as "believing you can eat the rooster that scratches over your grave."

I think he is right. I constantly remind myself that patience and tenacity are the keys to winning! It is the practical application of the biblical admonition to ". . . run the race with patience. . . ." You are going to experience exhilaration, discouragement, overwhelming fatigue. Just don't quit! Rest and rally!

Personally, I like the man who built a stone wall around his house six feet wide and four feet high. Someone asked him why he had built a wall that was wider than it was high. He replied, "Because, if it ever blows down, it'll be higher than it was before it blew down."

We have to plan that way. We must plan our commitment to marriage so that storms and other disruptions make it taller and stronger than before. We must marry for better or worse, for richer or poorer, in sickness or in health! Perhaps Margaret Mead was right when she observed, "The most serious thing facing America today is people entering marriage thinking it temporary."

It is not temporary! Perpetual, uninterrupted happiness is temporary! Marriage is forever! We must constantly remind ourselves, because of the adverse regular and subtle impact of subliminal stimuli, that joy and elation in marriage are temporary. Fatigue and cowardliness in marriage are temporary! Optimism and pessimism are both temporary. These too shall pass! Marriage is forever if it is to work at all.

In short, we need to remember the "institutional rule" of chapter one. "Changing institutions (banyan trees or marriage partners) does not compensate or facilitate." In other words, marrying someone else does not necessarily correct the problem. We may be simply leaving the one who loves us the most and who might have helped us the most. We trade them in on another only to be surprised that we reach the same point of fatigue sooner and with more intensity than before. It's the same song, second verse, should get better but will probably get worse. It will probably keep getting worse until we handle the real problem, scratch where it itches, and stop running away from it under the guise of running *to* something else.

A member of my church sent me a "Dear Abby" column that illustrates my point. It read:

> Dear Abby,
> Regarding letters from "the other woman," so far you have printed only letters from women who were dumped. How about a letter from a "winner"? My married lover left his wife for me!
> I was told that I wasn't breaking up anything; his marriage was dead long before he even met me. His wife had gotten fat. I was married, too, but I assured him that my marriage was also over—my husband had gotten dull and boring.
> So I divorced my boring husband and he divorced his chubby wife. Oh, yes, we both had children, but we explained that we were in love and when they were older they would understand.
> Our marriage was a dream come true. No more lying and sneaking around. At long last we were legally man and wife, for all the world to see.
> Our apartment was filled with modern furniture and old-fashioned guilt. And plenty of doubt and mistrust.
> Two years later he was meeting someone new. I told him he was a liar and a cheat. He said it took one to know one.
> And by the way, he's gotten a little dull and boring, and I've put on a little weight.*

---

* Taken from the Dear Abby column. Copyright, 1982, Universal Press Syndicate. Reprinted with permission. All rights reserved.

She signed her letter, "A Winner!"

There are winners and there are quitters, but there are no winners who are quitters! Patience and tenacity, even in the face of fatigue, equal success.

Recent studies by Blood and Wolfe in *Core Concepts in Health* seem to substantiate this premise. This study shows that after one year of marriage 98 percent of the wives interviewed believe they had married the right man. After two years of marriage that number dropped to 56 percent. At twenty years of marriage the number dropped to an unbelievable 6 percent who felt they had married the right man. But, when the surveyors began talking to people who had been married twenty years or more, the interviews revealed that 95 percent of the women questioned believed they had married the right man.

Patience and tenacity are the keys to success in anything. Hang in there and don't quit! You will want to. Everyone lucky enough to be part of a dynamic relationship will experience fatigue; and fatigue makes cowards of us all. Don't quit! Fatigue is natural and we need to scratch that until it feels good again and go on with the job of growing up together.

Ruts and Routines

The second of the most common internal causal factors of marital discomfort is sameness. People may articulate this irritant in different words and modes, but it all translates, "We got in a deep though comfortable rut and smothered."

Now, if changing banyan trees or partners is *not* the answer, what is? The answer is, change ruts or sameness—not the partner!

This factor, the destructive addiction of sameness, reminds me of the story of two frogs (let's say Mr. and Mrs.) making their umpteenth trip down the same path to the same pond. Mr. Frog fell into a deep rut and try as he might, he could not get out. Mrs. Frog, standing above the rut, admonished, cajoled, beckoned, and belittled. "Get out, come on, let's go," she pleaded.

Mr. Frog, down in the deep rut, said simply that he couldn't. "I've tried everything and there is no way I can get out of this rut."

Mrs. Frog hopped on down to the pond, and in a few minutes Mr. Frog appeared beside her on their favorite lily pad. "I thought you said you couldn't get out," she exclaimed.

He responded, "Big truck came along and I had to."

That's the critique of the sameness factor! We *have* to get out of our comfortable, lethal ruts. A big truck is coming down the road and it will crush our relationship. The problem is not so much with the partner as it is staying on the same path to the same pond. Changing partners is not generally the answer because we tend to take *them* back to the same path and pond that we are used to. By doing this, we try to prove, at least to ourselves, that our original problem was not internal (me) but external (her!).

The word I used for this factor in an earlier chapter was *burnout*. Burnout comes from sameness not from intensity or pressure. We burn out when we are so repetitive that we create boredom. Thus, burnout is peculiarly unique to good jobs, good leisure pursuits, and especially, good marriages. In good marriages we tend to repeat what we enjoy, and the constant repetition, without variation, cuts deep grooves in the record and often destroys the melody.

Move about *in* the relationship. Explore new paths and different ponds together. Plan together to broaden the scope and horizon of the relationship. Jointly plan to scrupulously avoid sameness. No matter how much you enjoy doing something the same way, sameness eventually degenerates into staleness. Move about!

I see this principle illustrated most often in sexual problems within the marriage. I spoke with a couple not long ago who had evidently enjoyed great sexual satisfaction and gratification in their long marriage. They had come to see me because this great communication and affirmation bond between them had suddenly and frighteningly become stale. I encouraged them to tell me about their life together in general and their sex life specifically.

They were still in love. They had an amazing grasp of what was and was not normal in their feelings and frustrations. They adequately perceived the subliminal input of the audio/video media of our day. They were not threatened by normal fatigue or predictable, healthy boredom.

They were beset with sameness! Their sex life had become so routine and predictable it was now one deep rut. They had played this favorite tune with such enjoyment and appreciation that the needle had cut a groove so deep the very life of the record was threatened. Theirs was a case of same room, same bed, same approach, same position, same sameness! Burnout was setting in.

I encouraged them to move about! I encouraged them to at least try a different room. Have sex under the back porch, in the rose garden, swinging from a tree, do something differently! They did, though I feel sure they did not find the tree suggestion very helpful except to make the point of variation. Their rediscovered pleasure and affirmation taught them (as all wise couples should try to remember) that it isn't necessary to change tunes, and certainly not instruments, but it is necessary to experiment with variations in the expression of that tune.

Speaking of sex and sameness, this same dynamic is often behind the so-called "black nightie syndrome." Often I have heard a distraught wife say, "My husband has become a dirty old man! He wants me to wear all these slinky, black things, and I don't know what's going on."

What is *often* going on is a loving husband's subconscious awareness that sameness kills. It may be one person saying to another, "Dress so that I know I am important to you. Don't keep looking the same and for goodness sake, don't dress or undress as though I were not real."

Sometimes this change of scenery or this moving around is not something totally new. As often as not, it may be a simple reaching back. Most couples I see have been married about fourteen or twenty-one years. Many times I help them scratch through the sameness itch by reaching back. They met on a tennis court, loved playing tennis throughout courtship, and haven't been on the court together in ten years! For others, reaching back may be surfing, the theatre, flower shows, and so forth.

About the twenty-first year of our marriage, Sandra and I felt the need to reach back in order to move on. For us, reaching back meant camping. When we were first married and as our children were growing up, we had experienced many wonderful times in the woods together. As our two boys entered adolescence, we purchased a summer house in the Cumberland foothills of Tennessee and stopped camping entirely. In our twenty-first year of marriage our children were grown and on their own. We needed our old bond. We purchased a small tent trailer. For a period of about two years we once again enjoyed nature together. We have since sold our camper, are still enjoying our Tennessee farm, and are currently working on a new project that promises variation on the same great theme.

One of the major causes of burnout and one of the mortal ene-
mies of variation is postponement. Many of us have known this
problem well. We succumb to the tendency to say, "Wait until
the kids are in college; wait until the kids are through college; wait
until . . ."

Do something special and different together and do it now!
There's always a good reason to wait. But there are better and less
obvious reasons to do some things at this moment in time. This is
not an admonition to do away with prudent saving. It is but an encouragement to not live constantly for tomorrow. Habitual postponement is lethal for it is one more form of sameness that can
eventually culminate in burnout.

Sameness, not great family traditions and rituals, but *sameness* is
a gigantic and lethal internal factor! We can and must learn how to
cultivate family patterns without creating destructive routine. We
can and must acquire the fine art of knowing how to create "one-
ness" without fostering "sameness."

Mid-Life Crazies

The third of the three most common internal factors that cause
discomforting itch in marriage is the so-called mid-life passage
through which, if we're lucky, all of us must journey. Call it what
you may—menopause, premenopause mentality, mid-life crisis, or
middle-age crazies—the reality exists for both sexes.

The onset of this period tends to be viewed by our culture as totally negative. We hear such quaint phrases as "over the hill,"
"middle age," "the big Four-O" and "going through the change."
While the occurrence is a demanding and disruptive internal factor
for most marriages, it can be, if scratched right and dealt with, a
normal door to a new beginning. The point is, as with all irritants,
to scratch where it itches not everywhere else. See such normal,
predictable marriage problems through! Menopause, mid-life adjustments for the husband and the wife, is one of these internal
challenges.

I treat this important factor with some brevity because this is an
area of research receiving quality attention by qualified experts.
Volumes of books and pamphlets are now available to the serious
reader, giving practical aid to both men and women struggling with

this stage in their marriage. I list it and comment on it briefly because it *is* one of the three most common internal factors affecting marital bliss and maturation.

While men do not go through all the physiological changes in mid-life that women do, they do, nonetheless, experience with their wives changing body, changing mind, changing world view. These changes, forced on any couple by the march of time, can be just as real and potentially devastating to men as to women.

In point of fact, men do not tend as a general rule to handle their mid-life course adjustments as well as does the *average* woman. Their track record might even support the allegation made by some counselors that men are actually the weaker sex!

For instance, there are three basic steps to be found in emotional problem solving. After a suitable period of denial, step one is to initiate the crisis. That is, bring the problem out into the open so that it must be dealt with. Step two is coming to the realization of what one must do about the problem. Step three is determining how we go about doing what we've decided must be done.

Men caught in something as subjective and threatening as the mid-life crisis are longer on denial, quicker on initiating the crisis, and inevitably move too quickly to settle the issue.

Women, on the other hand, experiencing the same disconcerting psychological threats are less prone to lengthy denial. They initiate the crisis less dramatically and potentially less destructively. More importantly, they tend to pause longer to explore fully the two final stages: what should be done and how to go about doing it.

This is strength! Men may be able to benchpress 300 pounds, but real strength is the ability to live in suspended animation. Real strength is the poise that allows us to open a thing up and deal with it as opposed to blowing a thing up and getting it out of one's hair.

Put another way, I am simply stating the clinical fact that for every twenty-five marriages in trouble the counselor may see three of the twenty-five husbands while seeing all twenty-five wives. The *average* man tends to say such things as: "Don't lay any of that mid-life crisis junk on me!" "I know who I am. I know what I am doing. You need the help, not me."

The evidence I have observed leads me to believe that it is the husband who tends to make the most foolish mistakes, based on the poorest perspectives, and pursued with the greatest vigor. This, and not the inevitable psychological or physiological changes, is what constitutes the greatest source of danger for the marriage. Women can blow it, and often do, but men hold the crown. Both must concentrate more creative effort toward a solution.

Working together is imperative because that is the way any problem in marriage is solved. Women may be stronger in general because they have a distinct advantage. Not only have they been constantly forewarned about this development in life, but they also have more distinct and unmistakable physiological factors on which to blame their psychological fluctuations. Men, at least until recent years, tend to be less warned and see little physical evidence that they are entering a new passage.

Both husband and wife, however, experience many of the same emotional symptoms of the passage. Some of the more common bisexual symptoms are: depression, unpredictability, uncontrollable moods, irritability, indecisiveness, fluctuating self-esteem, crisis of confidence in one's self or in the marriage.

These symptoms may express themselves in various ways. One partner may start looking for "someone who understands me." Others experience what one counselor calls "a spasm of readolescence." Some may exhibit a proneness toward linen shirts, open collars, something rather macho dangling on their hairy chest (women excepted). Some buy a new sports car they can't afford. All of these are signs that simply warn us to stop, think, and scratch where it itches.

One further reflection on menopause, as I use the term so generally. While many of the accompanying symptoms must be overcome, overwhelmed, ignored, or simply survived, still others are medically treatable. Much is being done today, for instance, in hormone replacement: both estrogens and androgens. New attention is being given to vitamin E supplementation. Regular checkups have always done much to circumvent or correct physical maladies in both men and women, and many moods and disorientations have physical causes.

Another relatively new area of interest, another way to scratch where this itch is found, is increased emphasis on knowing how to care for oneself. Physical exercise, good food, and healthy emotional stimulation are now coming into their own as important factors in alleviating some forms of mid-life discomfort.

Whatever the treatment and whatever the proper term for describing this time in life, both husband and wife must be aware. One of the leading causal factors in marital discomfort is what I have generally labeled menopause.

The point of this and the previous chapter is that you are going to itch! There simply is no relationship that does not present normal, natural times of test, trial, and evaluation. Such times are indeed necessary for strong maturation and must be approached with appreciation and wisdom.

These stressful periods of irritation may not come in nice, neat seven-year increments. Your itch may be a day late or a year early. Be assured, however, if you have entered into the process of growing up with someone else and are attempting to develop a mature marriage, you are going to itch. As you develop a mature marriage, you are going to itch. As you develop a beautiful and solid relationship with your partner, you will experience periodic discomfort. The rule is hang in there; scratch where it itches and grow up wisely.

CHAPTER 7

Intimacy: Trouble With the Thermostat

> Adam and Eve were in different parts of the Garden of Eden when the Lord commanded Adam to go and squeeze Eve's hand.
> "What's a squeeze, Lord?" Adam asked.
> The Lord explained, and Adam went and squeezed Eve's hand. Then the Lord told Adam to kiss Eve. Again, Adam was confused and asked for an explanation, which was given. And Adam went off and kissed Eve.
> Then came the command for Adam to go forth and multiply.
> Before long, Adam was back. "Lord," he asked, "what's a headache?"*

From that alleged day to the present couples have had to learn to work together on the complex issue of sex. They have had to learn that sex is not a game people play but is a sacred drama of the heart. They have had to learn that sex is not "doing what comes naturally" but the natural doing of that which is mutually satisfactory and mutually affirming. It is exploring but not exploitation. Sex is the process of making the kind of love that engenders love making. It is special. It is sacred and it is fragile.

While this chapter concerns itself with the broader subject of intimacy in general, sex within marriage is highlighted specifically. This is done not only because sex is the first thing usually thought of when intimacy is mentioned but because sex, though it is only an aspect of intimacy, is also the trickiest and the timeliest. In highlighting it, but pressing on to broaden the study to include all forms of intimate interaction, I hope to foster the notion that "good inti-

---

* Lew Breyer, quoted by Alex Thien in the *Milwaukee Sentinel*, reprinted with permission from the *Milwaukee Sentinel* and from the February 1976 *Reader's Digest.*

macy" is much more than good climax in bed—that it is a reach beyond that to good climate in the home. Sex, or any other form of intimate interaction, is the mutual caring within the marriage that *creates* warmth and security for both partners.

Couples from Adam and Eve on have had to learn that sex is a special dynamic in the marriage relationship. It and other expressions of intimacy are the source of much of our marital joy and happiness and, sadly, so much of our marital misery and insecurity.

This is precisely why someone has wisely observed that intimacy within the home is both a thermometer and a thermostat. It measures the temperature of the relationship but, more importantly, it can *determine* the climate of the entire marriage. As a properly functioning and properly used *thermostat* this "instrument of intimacy" between husband and wife can literally change cold and frigid to warm and comfortable. Improperly used, it can also change warm and comfortable to cold and frigid! Thus, as we define the word *sex* to include all of the intimate interaction within one's marriage, we must see its capability for controlling the very *climate* of the relationship. Mature sexuality can act as a practical and effective thermostat. Immature or uninformed sexuality is a thermometer that registers the coldness of a deteriorating relationship.

Using this analogy as a place to hang our thinking caps, let us remember two things. First, due to a number of critical factors that will be explored in this chapter, most thermostats need adjusting, if not fixing, to one degree or another. Fortunately, it is quite possible in the vast majority of cases to make the necessary adjustments so that all intimate interaction within the marriage does more than simply measure the temperature of the home. Fortunately, with proper adjustment creative intimacy can seize the initiative and *determine* the very climate of the home!

Second, it is important to remember that two people are involved. Each partner comes to the potential of creative intimacy with their own preconceptions, misconceptions, perspectives, orientations, fears, and needs. Therefore, in order for this thermostat to function properly, the husband must work on his half of the instrument. The wife must work on her half of the instrument. And, both must work together on the whole!

Getting this thermostat to function creatively requires thoughtfulness and hard work on the part of both partners. Healthy climate-controlling sexuality is not an automatic process. In this chapter we will take the initial step of exploring some of the critical factors that tend to disrupt creative, climate-controlling intimacy. Chapter eight will cover some of the adjustments that can be made so that both partners can more effectively contribute to the care and maintenance of the marriage.

Mirror, Mirror on the Wall

Obviously the starting place for evaluating the orientations and preconceptions that may need adjusting is our own early childhood. We do tend to reflect the models we have observed. We may copy these models precisely as observed (positive imitation) *or* react just the opposite (negative imitation). Either way, we tend to mirror our early models. We are inclined toward imitation whether it is just like, or precisely unlike. Either is imitation!

As we assess our half of the thermostat, the ability to control climate within the marriage, we must ask some critical questions. What did I first observe concerning intimacy in my earliest role models? How have I copied that inadvertent or deliberate instruction? How is my imitation affecting my adult relationship now? Has it, is it disrupting my ability to live within my marriage in a climate-controlled atmosphere of warmth and comfort?

Answering these questions not only gets us back in touch with the old tapes playing in our subconscious but also helps us correct the tune to which we may presently be dancing. In addition, exploration of *our* earlier models (or lack of models) while our partner does the same with *their* background can also help both husband and wife appreciate the multiple influences impacting on their adult and mutual relationship.

This multiple influence is what has caused at least one researcher to comment that when a husband and wife go to bed for the purpose of sex there are *four* in that bed! There is his mom and dad and there is her mom and dad all in varying degrees of impact and presence. This is, of course, but another way of picturing our ever present early-childhood orientations.

However, the couples I have talked with lead me to believe there are actually a minimum of *six* in bed! There is the husband and his mom and dad and there is the wife and her mom and dad. All six are crowding the situation in varying degrees. All six are reacting to and influencing this critical moment of intimacy. This crowded situation may have been what prompted Aldous Huxley to describe sexual intercourse as ". . . a maniac struggling in the musky darkness with another maniac." While Huxley may really only be telling us of the inadequacy of his own sex life, he is also reminding us of the *thermometer* aspect of intimacy. He reminds us that intimacy can, as in his case, depict rather than determine that the atmosphere is healthy or unhealthy, comfortable or miserable. For us, however, we seek the fully functioning *thermostat,* the creative control of climate. Therefore we press on in our evaluation of the crowded bed, the lingering effect of early childhood role models.

Decongesting this bed requires that we begin at our beginnings. We can best evaluate what is happening now, or ought to be happening now, by reevaluating where it all began.

We might rhetorically ask these parents who crowd and impact our beds: What did you teach me by words, attitudes, or actions about sex being beautiful and sacred? Or, did you program me to feel that sex is dirty, sordid, or demeaning? Did I learn to *use* sex or other forms of intimacy as tool, weapon, or source of leverage in my marriage? Did I enter into sex or intimacy with an attitude of affirmation and caring or self-indulgence and crassness? Did you teach me, whether deliberately or not, that sex is an endurance contest? Or did you help me appreciate it as an endearment opportunity?

If intimacy within the marriage is not contributing to enhancing the warmth and health of the relationship a good percentage of the time, we may need to begin at the beginning in order to locate the fundamental disruption. Mirror, mirror on the wall . . . what can you tell *me* about *me?*

Diamond in the Scuff

Of course, parents are the first influence on our orientation toward sex specifically and other forms of intimacy in general. But, let's not dump everything on poor mom and dad! *Society* has taken many a well-polished, carefully cultivated gem and pressured it and scuffed it back into black coal. The parents did their best, society destroyed the sparkle! When one leaves the nest, there is a cold and sometimes-ruthless world out there waiting. The ruthlessness of our society *and* foolish choices made by the child conspire at this stage to disrupt the thermostat so necessary to later marriage.

As we seek to adjust the intimate interaction of our marriage, we must look at the impact that our social environment (today) has had on our attitudes and preconceptions. We must, for instance, critically evaluate society's input when it advocates "free love." If not, we are destined to discover the hard way that such intimacy is neither free nor is it love.

When society speaks of the sexual revolution, the implication of this phrase is evolvement for the better. It is supposed to indicate that we have finally reached a point in history when puritanical straitjackets have been stripped away and a *new* and *better* day has arrived.

Critically evaluating this concept may preserve the potential of creative intimacy in our marriage. It may reveal that the day is not new at all—that men, in their crass chauvinism, have traditionally undressed women and treated them as objects until they become bored. Then, they begin to dress them again, to regain some sense of titillation, so the cycle can be repeated.

This utilitarianism, which condones using someone as you would a common utility, is an age *old* scuff by society. It tends to distort the attitudes and perspectives that one has toward sexuality and intimacy. And, when this piece of programming is brought unchallenged into marriage, it will disrupt creative intimacy and cause much pain.

Not only is today's so-called sexual revolution not new, it's not better! Granted, we have gotten rid of some certified rubbish that should have been thrown out long ago. But, if you will listen closely to the claims of the sexual revolution, it does not even claim to be better! What it claims is great beauty at no cost! It claims marvelous value at slashed rates. It teaches and advocates the quest of maturity through blatant immaturity! In fact, marriage counselors all over are discovering that as the sexual revolution progresses (if that is the right word), problems with sex in marriage grow proportionately! I see an increase yearly. Other counselors report the same observation.

One of the reasons sexual problems increase in direct relationship to the intensity and duration of the so-called sexual revolution is that it gives us a false and unrealistic picture of intimacy. It doesn't prepare us for the tough job of putting our partner first. It does not help us appreciate the need for tenderness, thoughtfulness, and togetherness. Much, if not most of what this model teaches is inaccurate or half true. For instance, when was the last time you witnessed a torrid love scene in glorious technicolor on your TV or at the movies, and just at that point of tantalizing ecstasy the girl stops and says, "Wait a minute! I've got to go to the bathroom first"? That's reality! Physical needs, emotional orientations, personal drama, and complicity and complexity are seldom portrayed. The pictures given us by the sexual revolution are simply not very accurate and are thus disruptive to our thermostat, creative intimacy. These pictures simply leave people feeling inadequate, inferior, or perhaps just different.

If we look objectively, we can see where our society, with its influence and impact, can disrupt our marriage. Let's go on to another even more potentially devastating factor emanating from our society.

Titillation Without Representation

One of the demanding factors that can be brought into a marriage is what the husband and wife may remember or may have experienced in their teenage years. Recalling this initiation can help marital intimacy. This initial encounter with sex can very much affect our adult world.

Adolescence is a period when interest in and desire for physical contact with the opposite sex is evolving and exploding. And in our day opportunities to explore or exploit this emerging drive are numerous. Along with this, sexual stimulation in the environment is continual, and the average teenager is not yet emotionally equipped to deal with it all.

This needed equipment, known as emotional stability, comes to the average person at around age twenty-five (give or take a year or three). I know one guy who is eighty-seven and doesn't have it yet, but we speak of the *average*. Emotional maturity is the emergence of our more stable and more mature adult.

Without this more dependable adult, and given the saturating bombardment of the senses experienced by today's average adolescent, we have what I call titillation without representation! It is this constant stimulation of the *vulnerable* teenager that can cause disruption in future intimate interaction.

For one thing, when the *boy* has been to Paris it is hard to get him back on the farm! The same is true of the teenage *girl.* Such an early trip can be disruptive. Adolescents are tantalized, stimulated, and opportunized before they are ready, and at no cost to them in commitment or responsibility. As they later assume the commitments that lead to mature intimacy in marriage, there must be some evaluation and readjustment. This too-much-too-soon exposure is one reason both husband and wife need to explore their adolescent sexual orientations and disorientations.

Most teenagers have not achieved complete emotional stability. It's still a few years away. Therefore, our society's preoccupation with sex and compulsiveness in sex can be disruptive. Many young people later find that too much sex too soon is actually translated play now, pay later.

Put another way, vulnerable, highly impressionable adolescents are capable of doing things they are not yet prepared to handle. They are quite capable of feeling excitement—in fact, cheap, easy, high excitement—without the ability to understand the impact this easy and irresponsible exposure can have on their adult relationships. There may follow a reluctance to make necessary adjustments in marital intimacy. Put simply, it was so easy and without demand *then,* why is it not still the same *now?*

If adolescence is a period when one is exposed to things prior to emotional stability (titillation without representation) then we need to look briefly at the law of diminishing returns as it affects one's marriage.

When this law is stated formally, it usually reads: In all *ego* centered activity one must *increase* the *stimuli* in order to maintain the *original* response. If we deformalize it and apply it to dating, we would say, if what you are doing is for *self* then you have to keep doubling the dose just to keep the same feeling you had when you started out.

For example, if your goal in life is to be a millionaire just for self-gratification and pleasure then you are in the grips of that law. You make your first $100 at age fifteen and are *thrilled!* Then, it takes $200 just to create the *same* thrill. If you persist in self-centered preoccupation, you will need $400, then $800, up till the first million, just to feed the original fire. Then, having made $1 million, two is needed to keep the same feeling! On and on it goes, insatiable and unending!

If you'll look back at your dating in adolescence, you may find this same self-centered problem. We dated people in high school not because it made *them* feel good but because of what it did for *us!* At this age and state this is not only natural but is also healthy.

But, then we got married and may have failed to change gears. Dating and marriage are not the same. Most people recognize this, but many fail to make the change that indicates that we *really* recognize it. We tend to continue trying to meet our needs when we very much need to shift to concern for the needs of the person we have married. The changeover from ego-centered dating to other-centered marriage, and all the implications thereof, is unrehearsed and often so very hard to handle. Adolescence, in a way, is practice for the real thing. Marriage is the real game. Any coach will tell you that a team *plays* the way it *practices.* Take a close look at your adolescent experiences that may be affecting your marriage now.

At least one other aspect of the adolescent's sexual awareness should be mentioned. It is an unwritten rule that every boy knows intuitively. I say boy because I mean boy! Girls, as a rule, do not understand this and tend only to find out about it too late.

The rule? Adolescent boys, even in this day and time, do not tend to marry the person with whom they have been intimate. The primary reason for this appears to be that in adolescence the average girl is more mature than the average boy and therefore leans toward permanence as a result of intimacy. He, on the other hand, being characteristically less mature, tends toward a lessening of interest when intimacy destroys the mystique.

A possible effect on marital intimacy of all this can be a tendency on his part to "love 'em and leave 'em." She, on the other hand, may have become so conditioned to touch and pleasure followed by being used and dropped that her ability to function properly in a marital relationship can also be hampered by her earlier experiences.

For instance, I often hear a wife say that every time her husband sits by her side on the sofa and holds her hand, she expects to be dragged eventually to the bedroom. Many of these women are not necessarily dealing with the present situation but are reflecting adolescent scars of touch and pleasure followed by use and abuse. Obviously, the average woman expressing this sentiment is not complaining about her husband's wanting to hold her hand. She is but responding to the erratic function of her adult thermostat due to abuse in earlier years.

Thus, because of this previously mentioned rule, our dating experiences in high school need to be explored. He *may have* become a practiced manipulator. She may *unfairly* suspect that he is just manipulating! The husband and the wife may need to search back along lovers' lane or at the drive-in to discover why ideas and suspicions exist in their adult relationship.

Every marriage possesses the potential for determining, not just registering, but *determining* the climate of the home. *This potential* is what I call the thermostat. This potential for determining the climate of the marriage can be disrupted by one or a combination of several periods in our movement toward marriage. Early childhood models can cause disruption or even malfunction. The influence and input of our society can create problems. We can also lose some adult skills for determining our own climate because of how we treated one another, and were treated, in high school. And, as if that weren't enough, there is another phase in our passage that can cause very real trouble in our eventual ability to *determine* the climate of our marriage.

Countdown to Marriage

While the adolescent years can cause a lot of trouble in a future marriage, the problems are by no means over when a person hits mature dating years. I define this time as the period between the earliest signs of the arrival of emotional stability and the time when one should possess this important asset (roughly the college-age years).

People who look back from twenty years or two years of marriage rather rapidly see how critical and formative this latter period has been on their marriage. If this is true, then our experiences and exposures during these mature dating years need some assessing if we would increase our capacity to control the climate in our marriage through creative intimacy.

One of the major effects of the countdown period is how your emotional experiences *then* affect your marriage *now*. Dating is a highly insecure time when contrasted to a safe and secure marriage, and emotions are different in each situation. The more insecure we are in a given situation the more sensitive and responsive are our emotions. As we become secure in a situation—in this case marriage—we become less sensitive and responsive.

This principle is easily observed in everyday life. All about us we see how sensitive and responsive our emotions are under stress and how this sensitivity and responsiveness diminish when security comes into the picture. For instance, we drive our automobile through mad traffic congestion and are threatened and intimidated from all sides. Then, we arrive home. We find ourselves safe and secure before our own familiar and friendly surroundings. Now the same emotions in the same person change. They automatically revert to a normal state, and at the same time we are not as sensitive and responsive as we were when our emotions were inflated and superalert.

The same principle holds in our more secure dating years and in the relative security of solid, legal matrimony. Our emotions change in *ease* of sensitivity and responsiveness. While dating we are easily alert, feeling, and sensitive. After the honeymoon we are not as easily responsive and are not as automatically on guard. Thus, before the marriage he will open the door for you. After the marriage he may begin driving away while you still have one foot on the curb. It is clear that the emotions are different and affect us differently. We can see the difference in observing that our house is on fire as opposed to enjoying a cozy flame in the fireplace. Our emotions are different and affect us differently when we are insecure as opposed to when we are finally secure. In dating she may respond strongly to his every touch but in marriage leave him feeling he has lost all his magnetism. The difference is not the people but how circumstances affect their emotions. Insecure situations make it *easy* for us to be sensitive and responsive. Secure situations reduce that ease.

Now by definition a good marriage is a secure marriage. And, if security does reduce the ease of sensitivity and responsiveness, then this very security can become one of our greatest dangers. Because we are secure, we begin taking each other for granted and problems begin to appear that are unique to good, secure relationships. It is this security followed by diminished emotional sensitivity that seriously tampers with our thermostat of creative intimacy. We are no longer *easily* attuned and responsive to each other and so we must now *work* at it!

If we do not work at it, we lose interest in appearing attractive to our spouse. We may not strive as hard as we once did to please this special person in our life. We may miss some nuances, needs, and opportunities in our marriage simply because we are no longer easily sensitized or responsive. If we do work at caring for and maintaining these important traits, then we can control the climate within the home and continue to enjoy the benefits and thrills we knew in our dating years.

You remember! Before marriage he was quite capable of looking dreamingly into her eyes. No words were needed. She knew she was loved. After marriage he often finds this awkward. This is not because he has changed his mind about her, but because his emotions have changed and his sensitivities and responsiveness are correspondingly diminished. Now, he cannot *easily* overcome his innate shyness or perhaps his early role models. He certainly needs to continue this affirmation, but now it takes an effort. The emotions have changed with the onset of security.

She has problems too. Before they were married, every time he touched her she moaned with ecstasy. Every time he kissed her she easily lapsed into hyperventilation! *She* totally convinced *him,* through her sensitivity and *responsiveness,* that he was the most magnetic dude on earth! Now that they are married, legally bound and secure, her attitude is more relaxed and so are her emotions. She hasn't changed in her feeling any more than he has, but now he perceives her as saying, "I'm willing to have sex with you, and would even like to, IF *you* can turn me *on.*" She, too, has allowed sensitivity and responsiveness to dwindle by default.

If both partners are mature, they will recognize the difference in the intensity of their emotions before and after marriage. They will work at keeping the imperative ingredients of sensitivity and responsiveness. If they do not keep these by working at it, they may both eventually feel used or abused. Then, with the return of insecurity, coupled with walls between them, each may foolishly turn to someone *else* to help them regain self-esteem or affirmation. Then, they may repeat the process again until finally, one day, someone awakens to the idea that natural emotions are the problem and that they must *make* THIS marriage work!

The application of this principle is practical and workable. Couples need simply to be aware that emotions are expanded and expansive in insecure situations and what they *easily* gave at such a time must now be *worked at* if the marriage is to remain secure.

One way to get a little further into the practical application of all this is to look at the situation in diagram form. This is an effort to picture what is *uniquely* happening to our emotions in *our day*. The diagram shows us that this mythical thermostat that can and must control the climate of our marriage is possibly more disrupted at the point of the mature dating years than at any other single point in our lives.

An experienced marriage counselor could be expected to draw a pretty accurate representation of what our emotions should look like in a normal situation of insecure dating and secure marriage. The problem, however, is that "normal" has changed with time and society.

But if this graph were drawn, it would look something like Figure 1 (and probably did look something like this around the turn of the century). A hypothetical couple getting married at 21 and 19 respectively, *without* the constant stimulation of emotions and opportunities for expression we now have, would approach their wedding day with their sexual feelings at a level appropriate to their age and not distorted by the impact of society. That is, he would be higher in his sexual interest because he is 21 and therefore right in the middle of this interest. She, on the other hand, being 19, would be somewhat below him in intensity because she is still five or six years away from her zenith period of physical need. After the wedding, if things were "normal," both would surge into higher excitability through the honeymoon period and then begin a slow tapering off of interest until he lost complete interest in sex at about age 102 and she at maybe 98. This normal-situation couple back then, or perhaps even rarely in our time, would be expected to have adjustments to make in their intimate interaction. But these adjustments were not and would not be as potentially destructive as they now are.

Figure 2 comes much closer to what is now the norm. Because of constant and perpetual stimulation of the emotions by TV, movies, magazines, and so forth, combined with social approval and inexhaustible opportunity, today's average couple approach their wedding day well *above* what is actually normal in stimulation and sexual expectation for their age. If they understand the practical application of the principle mentioned earlier, that emotions return to normal upon security, then they would *expect* not a rise in the honeymoon period (for many have already experienced this!) but a natural, healthy return to what is normal for their age (21 and 19). They would affirm this healthy adjustment to an unhealthy, over-stimulated world, and move on in time to the appointed loss of sexual interest at 102 and 98!

This is not what is happening, however! Figure 3 depicts the usual, run-of-the-mill, garden-variety problem experienced by today's couples.

Because of bombardment, brainwashing, naiveté and other factors, today's couple come charging into marriage, plunge to normal, compare it with "how it used to be" and grow farther apart. He accuses her of being frigid. It's the word he's been taught to say. She is finally convinced. He believes sex will fix any problem (the house can be on fire, the *bed* can be on fire, burglars can be in the closet, he can have sex!). Because he has a problem (the threat caused by the *normal* state of the emotions at the onset of security), he wants to have sex but she, characteristically, wants to talk. The more he wants to "fix things" by "being the way we were" the more she wants to talk. The problem grows until hurts become insurmountable and distances too great (*see* Figure 3).

This is why we hear so many couples say, "Before we got married, everything was GREAT! After we got married, BLAAAAAH!" They don't understand. They have not been informed. They do not know what normal is or how important normal is to solid *building!* How much better off they would be if they could be like the couple I saw the other day after six months of marriage. As the two of them passed through the door of my church one Sunday morning, she shook my hand and with a twinkle in her eye she said, "We have a new joke around the house now!" I said, "What is it?" As she took his hand she said, "We're now saying to each other, 'Did you notice the graph drop?'" Then they walked through the door, down the walk, holding hands, and laughing *together!*

How much better to appreciate the realities of normality, to affirm the imperative of building on secure foundations, and then work *together* to maintain sensitivity and responsiveness. Enjoy that togetherness all the way down to 102 and 98!

How much better our thermostats of creative, intimate inter-

SEXUAL ADJUSTMENT IN MARRIAGE

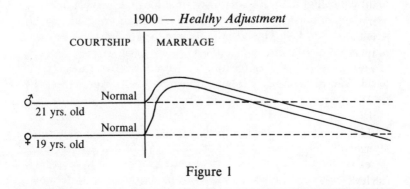

Figure 1

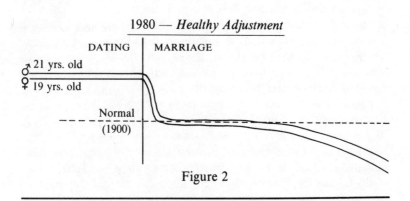

Figure 2

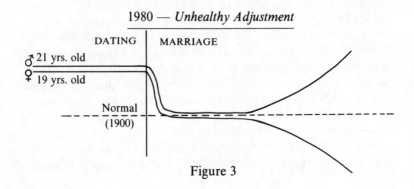

Figure 3

action *could* function if we knew better when and how they might have been disrupted. Kindly but critically evaluate the models of your earliest childhood. Be aware of the impact of society. Remember the awkward and overwhelming initial experiences you may have encountered in adolescence. Look at the emotions and their impact as the normality of bonded, secure love sets in. Finally, be aware of the following gremlins.

Miscellaneous Mischiefs

There are some miscellaneous mischiefs that can also disrupt our thermostat of creative intimacy. This list is probably quite long, but three surely deserve our attention. Any one of these three could be included under one or more of the sections already mentioned but perhaps can be better understood and assimilated as a miscellaneous mischief.

Sex will fix it is the first mischief or perhaps more accurately, the first myth. This mischief is a common idea held by many marriage partners and is primarily promulgated by the male of the species. The idea is that sex, per se, is a repair kit and will not only fix the problem we face but also make us as sensitive and responsive "as we once were." The notion is about as practical and sound as the one that says "what this marriage needs is a new baby"!

Sex won't fix it any more than a new baby will stabilize it. What is needed is creative intimacy, and creative intimacy may mean simply sitting together, holding hands together, crying together, and *talking* it out.

Climax is mandatory is the second most common mischief. This assumption, again, is primarily held by the husband. She *may* believe it due to brainwashing, but normally *he* carries this destructive baggage. He, or they, have been taught by the perpetual bombardment of the media that "great sex," the kind everyone supposedly has all the time, always culminates in great climax.

He buys into this misinformation more readily than she because this is, in fact, true for him. The male of the species does have to have a climax in order to experience full and satisfactory sexual gratification. He simply is constructed that way.

Not true of his wife! In fact, most researchers tell us that a woman who experiences full climax over 50 percent of the time is normal to above normal in response. Women are simply constructed *that* way! Many times during sexual intimacy a woman simply wants to be held, loved, and affirmed. Climax is desired at times but not all the time.

The commonly held idea that climax is always mandatory *always* causes obvious problems with creative intimacy. If he insists, for instance (because of his insensitivity, misinformation, or personal need), that she MUST experience climax then *society* is allowed to dictate the temperature of the marriage and not two caring people in love!

Not only this, he may ultimately convince her that she is somehow less a woman and thus further cripple creative intimacy. They really need to ignore or control the impact of "explicit adult situations in living color" and determine how *their* love should be expressed.

The clitoris is also a potential mischief-maker. The primary reason for this is that most people, if the reports are not misleading, do not know *what* it is and some evidently do not even know *that* it is!

The clitoris is that little nub of nerve endings at the top of the external female genitalia. It is this area that enables the female to experience climax when proper stimulation coincides with her emotional readiness. And, this clitoris is no problem for approximately 75 percent of all women. But, researchers are now saying that a staggering 25 percent (one-fourth of all the women in the world!) have a clitoris that is just enough out of position to make a climax during intercourse very difficult or impossible by normal friction only. When this fact is not known, as it *is unknown* to an unbelievable number of men and women today, there can be real trouble with the thermostat!

If this physical reality is understood and it is determined that she is of that 25 percent, loving care, tender understanding, and extra, simultaneous stimulation can put them both in charge of the climate of their marriage.

Incidentally and parenthetically, this factor is precisely why so many couples who are living together before marriage experience so much difficulty after marriage. Many of these women are of the 25 percent but do experience some climax before marriage. The reason they do is that they are living in insecurity, their emotions are expanded, and they are therefore more sensitive and responsive.

When normality sets in with security, and this must happen for solid building purposes whether they are in the 25 percent or the 75 percent category, all climax stops and the yawning gap pictured in Figure 3 becomes unbelievable in scope and speed of intensification.

Married couples, whatever course they traveled to bonded security, must be aware of the mischievous clitoris. One category, the 25 percent or the 75 percent, is not "better" than the other. It just means that people are different. Their physical appearance and appointments will vary and their emotional needs as well, and how those needs are met is just as varied. The point is that they must always work together for each other with each other to determine the climate of the home for *themselves!*

In this chapter I have attempted to state some of the leading problems that can adversely affect our thermostat of creative intimacy. I believe a practical understanding of these problems is critical because we need to know where we have been and how that may have affected us in order to know where we are now in our marriage. Having this knowledge we are better able to determine climate and not just register or react to climate.

In the next chapter we will explore some practical guidelines on how to readjust or reset this thermostat. We will keep working toward the important goal of deciding and determining our own climate within our own marriage.

CHAPTER 8

Intimacy: Resetting the Thermostat

In this chapter I want to talk to the "average couple." It may not necessarily be helpful to those occasional couples who need long-term marriage counseling, sexual therapy, or the attention of a good physician. The chapter is written for that majority of marriages which experience some varying degree of malfunction or disfunction of this climate-control mechanism, creative intimacy. Most married couples simply need sensitivity, determination, and *perspective.*

I list five helpful suggestions that can help us readjust our capacity for creative sexual intimacy. I have compiled this list from three basic sources. The first and most obvious is the twenty-five-plus years of my own marriage. Sandra and I have tried to function so that *we* could control the climate of our relationship and not just register the temperature created by external forces. I share from what we have learned together.

Second, this practical advice has been gleaned from many of the good articles and books being written in our day on the subject of marriage enrichment, care, and cultivation. We are all fortunate to have at our disposal much good material written by so many intelligent, literate, and sensitive people.

Third, this list comes from my experience with the hundreds of couples I have worked with who had a good thing going and learned how to keep it going. I have also learned much from couples who remind me of what *not* to do.

From these three principal sources I share this basic list of guide-lines on how to reset, repair, or readjust the thermostat. If the inti-mate interaction within your marriage is not in actual control of the climate of your marriage, these suggestions may help.

1. Be Aware of Nonverbal Communication

What you do in your marriage and how you act toward your marriage partner speak so loudly, your *words* are lost in the clatter! The couple who would help determine the climate of their home through their sexual or intimate interaction KNOW that mere words do not convey the bulk of the information perceived by their marriage partner.

Put another way, the plaintive cry "but I *told* her I loved her" will remain plaintive until we awaken to the reality that we are evi-dently not *living* lovingly! Mere words never offset the stark evi-dence of actual performance.

Philadelphia's Temple University has released a study that both supports and clarifies this particular guideline. This study shows that 7 percent of the message people receive from us (that is, what they actually think we are communicating) comes from the words we use! Just 7 percent! This revelation is incredible to ponder. It has profound implications for the preacher, teacher, employer, em-ployee, the husband, and the wife!

The Temple study goes on to show that 38 percent of the message we are actually sending out is conveyed to others by the *tone* of the voice. Therefore, verbally we may be saying, "I love you," while in reality we are communicating, "Please love me," "Pity poor me," or "I'm telling you what I have to tell you in order to get from you what I want to get!" The tone of our voice is more crucial in actual communication than are the words we use.

Further, the study states that a staggering 55 percent of the mes-sage actually received by the other person is completely *nonverbal*. The *majority* of what they perceive about us and about what we are attempting to communicate has nothing to do with either the words we use or the tone of our voice. An amazing 55 percent of what people hear and assimilate comes to them through facial expres-sions, posture, appearance, or other nonverbal "conspirators."

For example, a wife may verbally tell her husband that he is loved and appreciated, but in the simple act of never combing her hair *for him* she is *actually* communicating that he is taken for granted. When he says "all the right words" but is always sloppy in appearance or uncouth in manners, he may actually be communicating the same thing, "You are taken for granted."

We may be using the right words and managing a pleasing, supportive tone of voice, but that accounts for only 45 percent of what is received as valid data by our partner. Nonverbal messages convey more than words and tone of voice combined.

For instance, when she *says* she wants to make love but never looks enticing, she is verbally communicating her need for closeness but, at the same time, not letting him know that she cares a dime about his need for affirmation. Then she wonders throughout the night why he does not return her affections.

When he comes in and "wants sex" he may *think* he is telling her that she is loved, appreciated, and attractive. In reality, he very often communicates the fact that she fulfills the same basic need as a razor before breakfast or Gatorade after jogging. Then, he spends two pouting days wondering why she is not more responsive.

Most couples I talk with are ultimately amazed or aghast at what they are *actually* conveying to each other in their marriage. Most of them try to argue by exclaiming, "But I *said* so and so!" What we *say* conveys only 7 percent of the message being received. An overwhelming 93 percent of the actual message received by our partner comes to them through our tone of voice and our nonverbal statements.

This is one of the reasons some of our wisest counselors are now pointing out that good and meaningful sex is cerebral, not physical. It is thought through and then acted out. The *brain* must register such things as security and affirmation.

Good sex, or any form of climate-controlling intimacy, is not saying the right words and performing the proper act. Good sex doesn't come from great orgasm. Good and meaningful sex comes when both husband and wife *see* themselves affirmed, appreciated, noticed, loved. Sex and all forms of intimacy are primarily cerebral, not physical *or* verbal!

As Kevin Leman has suggested in his book *Sex Begins in the Kitchen,* a good healthy sexual relationship within a marriage begins at the breakfast table. It is at this point that money is put in the bank for later withdrawal. At the table at the beginning of the day, both husband and wife can begin to feel and understand that they are cared about. They are special, equal, and fun to be with. Good sex comes from early-morning courtesy and affirming appearance.

This is not to suggest that we can never let our hair down around someone we love. We all need to be comfortable and have that kind of relationship with someone. This is to suggest, however, that we can't go around in a constantly negative frame of mind and expect a positive environment. Negative breeds negative just as positive engenders positive!

Everyone needs to *know,* not to be confused with *hear,* that they are special, secure, unique, and loved. This is why it is so imperative that we become aware that MOST of what we are actually conveying is nonverbal.

Sex is communication! We must be consistently aware that we *are* communicating through all of our sexual words, attitudes, and actions. There is no greater forum for expressing affirmation or rejection of our husband or wife than through sexual intimacy. We "say" to our partner, "You are loved, respected, or important to my life." We clearly communicate that they are safe, secure, beautiful, and equal. We "speak" to them in a ringing voice that they are warm and attractive. Or, we communicate to them in no uncertain terms that they are ugly, utilitarian, a thing. Sex is communication!

This awareness is the first step in resetting or adjusting the thermostat. Caring for and maintaining a good marriage is very important. Very important to that concept is the need to have the kind of intimacy within the marriage that *determines* the climate of that home. Important to that concept is the need to be ever aware that nonverbal communication within the relationship may be drowning out our words!

2. Realize There Will Be Peaks *and* Valleys

This second guideline declares the obvious, that *all* marriages have high moments *and* very low times. If we are to keep our thermostats of creative intimacy functioning properly, we must know how to use this realization in practical ways.

An apt illustration of peaks and valleys occurred several years ago when our family was on summer vacation. We stopped in Nashville, Tennessee, to visit Opry Land, a large, sprawling entertainment and amusement park. As Sandra and I trooped through the gate with our two sons, David and Jimmy, I suggested that we make a trip around the park on a slow-moving train to get our bearings and plan our day. Jimmy, our younger son, joyfully announced that he planned to do just that but from the vantage point of the giant roller coaster that swirled through the park. He planned to zoom around the complex, above it, below it, enjoy the ride, and get to know the terrain all at the same time. He set out on his own and, for the most part, accomplished his goal. The rest of us took the train but due to flat, level travel were better able to see and assimilate the park. Unfortunately, perhaps, we do not have this same option in marriage. Marriage is a roller coaster. It is literally made up of slow starts, struggling climbs to the top, exhilarating heights, and sickening descents. We do not try to maintain *either!* We recognize both and are, hopefully, prepared for both.

What this means in practical terms is that if creative intimate interaction is to be maintained in the marriage, we should not allow our peak experiences to make us assume that valleys are either unnatural or deeper than they really are. By the same token, we do not allow the sickening descents to cloud the assurance that high experiences will come in due time.

Again, this is precisely what I talked about in chapter two when I quoted Richard Farson. "The better a marriage is the worse its partners will sometimes feel. It's a paradox we *must* learn to *live* with." Learning to live with it, the peaks and the valleys, is the meaning of intelligent assimilation.

When we do not *assimilate* this roller-coaster reality and constantly press for consistency, we not only spend a dreary day "chugging around the park," we also miss the opportunity to use our brain, to work *together,* and to mutually enjoy an exhilarating ride!

An unwillingness to accept a relationship that has peaks *and* valleys may be due to a naive notion that our parents seemingly had no such relationship. They were always in love! We never saw them squabble! Or, such unwillingness may mean that we demand our partner give us the constant and *easy* thrills we clearly remember from our dating years. A reluctance to recognize that both peaks and valleys are part of the ride may stem from a simple yet paradoxical fact: that this marriage has known truly great experiences; thus we find it difficult to settle for less in the same marriage. One thing is sure, however, pressing for consistency can obviously maladjust a thermostat that was designed to *cope* with a wild ride made up of exhilarating heights, scary descents, and frightening depths.

Pressing for consistency, especially in peak experiences, and not allowing for both peaks and valleys can seriously damage our ability to function *creatively* in marital intimacy. Some partners demand consistency with such determination that they will even settle for negative consistency. Constant valleys, for them, are better and easier to cope with than is contrast. If they can't have "it" all the time, then they'll settle for perpetual blah!

An unwillingness to recognize or adjust to peaks *and* valleys may simply reveal a need to revel in self-pity. This could stem from an unwillingness to forgive oneself or *accept* God's forgiveness for past failures. Demanding negative consistency as a substitute for positive consistency may mean many things to many people, but thermostats are designed for adjusting interior climate to exterior forces! We do not need to rationalize or be hard on ourselves or settle for unacceptable consistency; for while we cannot control the weather, we can do something about how it affects us. We can control the climate within the marriage if we can realize, accept, and cope with peaks and valleys.

This is precisely why this guideline is so important to proper climate control. We have very little to say about the rising and falling track our marriage seems destined to follow. But, with good sense and keen perspective, we can work together to make our marital environment healthy even when it cannot be just to our liking. Recognize that there will be peaks *and* valleys.

3. Minimize *Their* Programming

I salute the wife I read about who very intelligently handled another of today's disruptive influences on creative intimacy. Her husband, viewing her appraisingly, said, "You've got to do something about your figure!" "I have!" she responded, "I've thrown out all your *Playboy* magazines!" *

---

* By A. H. Dreyling. Reprinted with permission from the June 1972 *Reader's Digest*.

In a very meaningful way she was controlling the impact that "they"—meaning *anyone* or *anything* outside the marriage—exert on her marriage. She not only confronted this influence but also required her husband to do the same. What she was saying was that no one outside their marriage should be granted the power to dictate the climate within the marriage. "Their" (any outsider) programming must be controlled and curtailed.

It is important that all of us determine the climate of *our* home by pursuing sexual intimacy that is both uniquely ours *and* geared to the needs of both partners in the marriage (more on this in section five of this chapter). It is critical that we do not allow outside influences to inflict pain, pressure, expectations, or anxieties upon our marriage. We must critically evaluate what external programmers are attempting to tell us about intimacy and how we should feel and how we must perform or what we should think or do! This is not to suggest that we cannot learn anything from other sources. It is to suggest that we not allow ourselves to be harmfully programmed by other sources.

After all, and this bears remembering, much of society's input through movies, magazines, TV, and other forms of communication is oriented toward business prospects. It is primarily structured to make money, not to broaden and stabilize lives.

For instance, much of today's external programming rigidly affirms chauvinism. There is still, in our so-called enlightened times, a constant reiteration of the false idea that women are inferior playthings. We are constantly taught that sex is free and fun and holds no claim on responsibility. Marriage is temporary, so if you didn't luck out and find the right person the first time, then keep on looking.

Today's programming endeavors to project the idea that violence is acceptable outside the home *and,* more and more, inside the home. If your wife gets out of line, smack her! This, according to much of our current external programming, not only straightens her out but can also instill sexual passion. Today's programming regularly pictures adultery as not only acceptable but rather expected. It fosters immaturity, manipulation, and utilitarianism. It tends to demean tenderness, sensitivity, and permanence.

These influences can be fundamentally detrimental to all stable marriages primarily because we are allowing *external* forces to dictate the climate of *our* home. While it is true, as someone has observed, that you can't walk through garbage without getting some on you, it is equally true that we can minimize its stain if we are but aware of what we are having to walk through!

We must be critical! We must make evaluations. We do not have to accept everything we read, see, or hear. We can pick and choose if we do it with tough deliberateness. We can select and eject!

We must ask critical questions. Will this wash? Has this or will this idea or ideology stand the test of time? Is what I am being told to do or feel *someone else's* rationalizing or is it rational? If this concept has a *kick,* what is its *kickback?* Ask these questions and take an approach that will allow you to remain in charge of your own marriage.

If you think it through and determine to set your own climate in your own marriage, you may find that today's admonition of "free love" isn't free and isn't love. You may find that "playboyism" is but someone *else's* rationalization of their own life-style coupled with an effort to get your agreement so that they will feel better about what they are doing. Or, you may find this philosophy is not so much a way of life as it is a way for someone else to make money regardless of the cost to others.

Thinking never hurt anybody or any marriage and it may help you step around some very real garbage in our very disturbed society.

Creative intimacy in one's marriage, be it sexual intercourse, holding hands, caressing, or caring, must be determined by *that* marriage! No one, or thing, or influence must be *allowed* to come into *your* home and set or unsettle your climate. The climate of your home should be something mutually determined within your marriage. Then both partners must work together to have the kind of creative intimacy that is "we" and not "them."

Throw out the *Playboy* type of magazine if that's part of "their" intruding arm in your marriage. Or, perhaps it's your TV. I sincerely believe that some day sociologists or anthropologists will look back on our society, observe what we devour via our TV, and be amazed at what naive fools we were! Few intrusions are more real, more persistent, or lethal than television's not-so-subtle programming. It affirms affairs, encourages violence, and mocks morality. Control its control over you and your family and your marriage. In short, minimize outside programming.

4. Maximize *Your* Programming

Another way of fine tuning *our* sexual intimacies toward a healthier climate in marriage is to realize the necessity for *planning*. It isn't enough just to be aware of the lurking presence of outside influences. We must take some initiative and do our own programming.

I consider spontaneity an important ingredient in any good marriage. When married people are in love and are close and caring, it is legitimate to expect some things to just happen. There should be spontaneous love and spontaneous lovemaking. One should expect automatic warmth and marvelous serendipity.

However, if your marriage is to know creative intimacy, you need to plan for it and toward it. Make it happen! Choreograph intimate occasions between you and your spouse just as you would an important dinner for the boss, a family outing, or *anything* that is too important to be left to mere chance. Plan so that spontaneity has a chance and is nourished by *design.*

It constantly amazes me that couples who are alleged to be intelligent are so slow to appreciate the fact that some things, especially sexual opportunity and intimacy, must be planned for. In a world filled with pressure, unrelenting schedules, fatigue, and the patter of little feet, strategic planning is a must if a healthy climate is to be maintained.

The general assumption seems to be that if you do what "comes naturally" you will have a good, intimate, and healthy marriage. This assumption follows the one that says if you find the *perfect* person creative intimacy will just happen. No it won't! Good marriages are *made*, not discovered! They are earned, not bequeathed. They are created through thoughtful persistence and not delivered on a silver platter. Creative intimacy can be spontaneous but more often than not is lovingly choreographed.

For instance, when creative intimacy translates as sexual intercourse, much more attention must be given to "sex by appointment." I have encouraged many couples to adopt this more realistic approach, and it has proven to be a terrifically creative process.

Sex by appointment does not do away with spontaneity! It does not cause a couple to resemble the automated figures at Disney World. Quite the opposite in fact! This sensible approach can make the partners in the marriage even more aware that they are important—so desirable that pressure, fatigue, and children will not stand in the way.

I find that couples who plan for time together are actually more spontaneous than those who expect things to "just happen." Not only are they more spontaneous, they are certainly less frustrated and hostile. Their lovemaking generally takes on a rich togetherness not found in couples who demand constant spontaneity without programming.

If sexual gratification is truly cerebral, as many counselors allege, then two people planning together and working to *be* together play right into this theory. One of the most important ingredients of meaningful, intimate interaction, be it sex or holding hands on the backyard swing, is prior planning and imagery. Jumping in and out of bed is almost never conducive to the kind of warmth and growth that *determines* healthy climate. Spending time wanting to be together and planning to be together, however, excites the imagination and titillates the senses and determines a climate of affirmation.

Enjoy spontaneity when you are fortunate enough to have it pass by. But, if you are blessed enough to be married to someone very dear to you, and if you are as busy and buffeted as most of us are, you can do yourself and your marriage a big favor by being strategic! Plan, plot, and program togetherness *together.* Sandra and I have worked at doing this and have found, as have scores of other couples, that planning together gets you together. Not artificially and staged but warmly and lovingly.

We've looked at four practical ways to reset our thermostat. We must be aware of the power of nonverbal communication, be aware that good marriages have peaks *and* valleys and be prepared to handle both. We must always be on guard against the influence and programming of the *outside* world, which is not geared to building our marriage but to making money by pushing perverted values. We must always *work* on *creating* better opportunities for intimacy in our lives. And, of all the practical steps perhaps the most important is the fifth.

5. Be Other Centered

The fifth basic guideline for resetting our own climate-control mechanism, creative intimacy, is learning how to be *other* centered. It is a fundamental rule of God and man that the way to receive is to give. The way to find is to help someone else search. The way to stay fresh is to flow out.

This rule, like many others, is easier to say than do! Man, the egocentric animal, is not easily disposed toward being second. Be that as it may, being second is imperative in the care and maintenance of a good marriage. Thus, it is imperative to the proper function of the marriage thermostat, creative sexual intimacy.

The implication of this fifth principle is not that *I* have no rights. It is not meant to imply that I never have my place in the sun. It does not mean perpetual subservience, stifling sublimation, or crippling subjugation!

The meaning of this guideline is precisely what is taught by Jesus as recorded in the Gospel of Matthew *and* verified by life. Living creatively and positively by being other centered means, "He who seeks to find his life will lose it and he who seeks to lose his life for my sake will find it" (*see* Matthew 10:39). This is written in the Bible and is constantly corroborated by evidence in life!

People who make their own happiness the primary quest of their life seldom, if ever, find it. This treasure is usually unearthed by those who try to give happiness to others. People who try to find contentment and peace for themselves do not begin to come as close to these jewels as do those who endeavor to give contentment and peace to others. People who seek sexual gratification, or any of the varying forms of intimacy, for *themselves* almost never find it. But, those who endeavor with all their being to help their marriage partner know sexual gratification and fulfillment so very often find it for themselves!

There is a basic insatiability in self-centered preoccupation. It is a losing battle from square one. Self-preoccupation, for one thing, condemns one to live perpetually under the law of diminishing returns. Remember? This law dictates that we must constantly double the dose of whatever we do for ourselves, just to keep the original feeling we experienced when we began the process. Thus, money for self, sex for self-gratification, strokes for personal assurance, and all other forms of ego-centered activity are fundamentally insatiable because enough is never enough.

This is why, for instance, the forty-year-old playboy, the swinging single, and the jaded sophisticate can never get enough of *anything!* One dose must be followed by two doses, then four, then eight, then sixteen, endlessly, *just to maintain the original* feeling! The search is endless because it centers on ego-centered preoccupation.

It is this switch from self-preoccupation to other preoccupation that is the fundamental difference between dating and marriage. Dating is, by nature, self-centered. We do not date someone because of what it does for *them!* We date a specific person because of how that date makes *us* feel. Marriage, if it is to survive and if it is to mature in its beauty, must of *necessity* become other centered. Then, the law of diminishing returns, in all its insatiability, ceases to be operative as director and determinator.

We need to cease and desist from going about the home with our finger on *our* pulse saying, "How do I feel? How do *I* feel?" We MUST make the concerted effort to begin functioning in our marriage with our finger on *their* pulse saying, "How do they feel?" and "How can *I* help *them* feel better?" If you don't believe this, if it sounds like just so much platitudinous gibberish, try it! Cast your bread upon the water and you'll see. It *will* come back buttered!

Erich Fromm may have put it all in proper perspective in one of his more famous statements. Fromm taught us that we must learn to live together in such a way that our husband or wife will know that we need them *because we love them* and not that we love them because we need them. Other centeredness, ironically, is perhaps the shortest route to find what ego-centered persons search for so fruitlessly.

Obviously there are many factors that can and do disrupt the thermostat of creative intimacy in our marriage. But there are practical things we can do to reset or adjust this important thermostat if it has been disrupted:

1. Be sure your actions and your voice are carrying the same message as the words you are using. Live the way you talk and talk the way you live.
2. Enjoy the peaks and expect the valleys. Both are part of the same ride.

3. Control the outside forces that try to control you and your marriage.
4. Plan for and work toward things that are just too important to be left to chance.
5. Above all, get the most *by* giving the most. Put yourself first *by* putting your partner first!

CHAPTER 9

Communication: The Art of Getting Through

Clear and unhampered communication is one of the prime prerequisites in all areas of life! It's true if you are talking about the care and maintenance of a good job. We must remain in "common-union" with the task, the boss, and our fellow workers. The statement is axiomatic if one is speaking of caring for and maintaining a meaningful faith. Staying in touch with God through prayer has always been regarded as imperative in a strong spiritual life.

The need for good communication applies when one speaks of maintaining a good relationship with neighbors, taxi drivers, the grocer, anyone, anytime! Good, clear communication is certainly vital to the care and maintenance of a good marriage. Both husband and wife must consciously and conscientiously strive for common-union. This common-union of two people seeking to function as one is indispensable.

I speak now of communication, not information! While there is a place for information, the great need of a well-cared for marriage is acquiring the art of *getting through*.

If I am able to get through to my life's partner, then I have successfully transmitted to her or him my true and honest feelings, designs, and intentions. I have allowed my partner to peer into my soul and more fully appreciate my hopes and dreams. By doing this, I have at the same time given my husband or wife a better opportunity to help me clarify my goals and make them *mutual* goals. The two of us can now work toward them together. My partner knows where I am coming from and where I hope we can go as a couple. I have paid him or her the ultimate compliment of common-union. I have been open and loving enough to have gotten through, or attempted to get through, to them.

"Information" is quite different from that. Information is the process of informing, or serving notice. It does not ask for interaction or common-union. It does not tend to unify but tends toward unilateral movement. As the divorce courts will attest, many partners within a marriage often assume they have communicated when in reality they have only served notice.

As important as informing others can be, this chapter will concentrate on the all-important dimension of communication. It seeks to expand the skill that enables each person in the relationship to hear and be heard. What we seek is the prized skill that enables two people to live, plan, and progress in mutuality and respect. It seeks to encourage both the depth and degree of common-union.

Strangely enough, when a couple hardly knows each other, are in the process of dating or early engagement, communication lines seem very clear. Part of this is due to desire and hard work. This desire and hard work is aimed at guarding and controlling their individual "domestic personalities" (that little person still within us we looked at in chapter three) but also represents a deep consciousness of the need to bring their "social personality" to the front. They want to put their best foot forward. Each works at being civilized, mature in appearance, and sincerely interested in the other person. Thus, they inevitably enter marriage saying, "One great thing we've got going for us is the fact that we can communicate!" Communication doesn't seem terribly forbidding to most people, because all the necessary equipment is in place! With few isolated exceptions we all have the physical or physiological factors that enable good communication. We possess lips, tongue, mind, vocal cords, and vocabulary. Couples are using these instruments but often are not "getting through" because of static on the line. The trick, then, is to get the static off the line so that there can be clear common-union.

This chapter will concentrate on the two major roles of the *persons* involved. Chapter ten will explore the three most important *principles* involved in common-union.

Getting Through Starts With the Transmitter

At least one-half of the problem in getting a message through can be traced to the transmitter. The point of origin is critical in that messages garbled by the transmitter do not tend to clarify en route. There's the boss who asked her secretary why she had handed her a phone message that didn't make much sense. The secretary responded by saying, "I wrote it just like they said it!" The point of *origin* can be the source of confusion.

As people involved in developing the skill of clear communication, we must always remind ourselves that our partner will *probably* receive the message just as we stated it. The speaker, the transmitter, begins the communication process. What we *think* we said, *meant* to say, or *thought* we said is not important. What is important is how clearly we said it and what our *partner* heard us say. We must transmit with deliberate awareness.

It is the apparent lack of awareness of the need to transmit clearly that is one of the *unique* problems to be found in *good* marriages. I constantly remain intrigued, not so much with the reality that good marriages have problems just as do bad marriages, but that good marriages have special and unique problems. Good marriages know problems that are unknown in mediocre marriages, détente marriages, or out-and-out bad marriages.

"If We're So Close, Then You'll Just Know!"

One such unique communication problem to be found primarily in good marriages is the assumption of symbiosis. I use this technical word because it is being heard more and more in our society. And, it is the right word! We do tend to assume symbiosis. Loosely translated, *symbiosis,* or a symbiotic relationship, is the assumption that I am inside your head and you are inside mine. I know what you are thinking, and you know what I am thinking, therefore, communication is both automatic and clear.

Bad marriages do not tend to produce such naive assumptions. In a bad marriage we are more likely to hear, "Look, you dumbhead, here's what I'm trying to tell you!" Then, they proceed to *tell* them! They consciously *transmit!*

It is only in good marriages, solid relationships, that we find a marked tendency in couples to assume that they are so close, so in touch, that it is no longer necessary to consciously and conscientiously transmit one's thoughts and feelings.

Actually, only good marriages can afford such carelessness. They alone enjoy the luxury of assurance and security that generates the assumption of symbiosis. Their relationship is secure enough that they can afford to be presumptuous and careless. When we believe that our partner truly loves us and that they are understanding and solicitous of our feelings, then symbiosis seems implied and failure to consciously transmit becomes a real possibility. Rather than sending a clear signal, we expect them to discover our needs and intentions.

It is in this expectancy that we find one of the major sources of static on the line. The better a marriage is the *more* affirmation we come to *expect*. Assuming that we do have a symbiotic relationship, we ultimately demand 100 percent affirmation. That is, love me enough, know me enough, be solicitous enough of my needs that I no longer have to talk to you. I no longer have to consciously transmit because with us it just isn't necessary. This is a source of severe static!

Again, poor marriages are not in the least bit plagued by the assumption of symbiosis. Those in poor marriages accept the fact that the partner probably doesn't understand, maybe doesn't *want* to understand, or perhaps has only their own best interest in mind. For this reason, people in poorer marriages often *transmit* their true feelings and needs more clearly than do those in better marriages. In a good marriage there is a tendency to assume that each is so close to the other that they "just know" each other's thoughts and feelings. There is no such assumption in poorer marriages.

In a poor marriage, for instance, a partner pretty well knows that the only affirmation they are going to get is what they *create*. Therefore, if the partner needs sexual affirmation, they are prone to *say*, "I want to have sex. Take off your clothes and get in bed!" If they are hungry, they may say, "Fix my dinner *and* fix such-and-such just to let me know you care a little." If they want a job done, they may say, "Mow the lawn; straighten up your closet," or some *articulated* directive. This straightforwardness doesn't necessarily mean they have better common-union than does the healthier marriage. What it does mean is that they know in their weak marriage they had better clearly state their needs, for their partner isn't close enough to them to "just know." It means that in a poor marriage if a partner is in need of attention or companionship, they are more prone to say, "Sit down and talk to me," and *not* assume symbiosis.

"Saying It Takes Away From It!"

This leads into another unique problem of communication within a good marriage and is closely related to symbiosis. Good marriages often lose clarity of transmission because of a subtle tendency toward expecting 100 percent affirmation. In good marriages we often fail to communicate clearly because we expect our partner to discover what we need or want *because* in this way we feel even more secure and loved! In a good marriage, if sexual affirmation is desired, we don't want to have to ask! Having to ask loses something for us. We simply expect our wife to dress titillatingly, and be solicitous and seductive. Her knowing when we want our favorite meal makes us feel even more loved and affirmed. If there is straightening up to be done around the house, we assume our spouse will *know* and will do it because we want it done, bringing us greater affirmation. If we are lonely and need idle chatting and companionship, we assume they should realize that and not have to be told.

One of the most common statements I hear from good marriages gone bad is, "If I've got to ask for it, I don't want it!" Too bad! Perhaps we could allow the poor marriages around us to teach us how important it is to vocalize, to *communicate*. Maybe we won't vocalize our thoughts in the way they do, but in the awareness they do.

Failing to be a conscious transmitter is, among other things, but another way of saying, show me you love me without my giving any instructions. Help me feel better about myself because of "spontaneous" love. Understand what I'm feeling without my having to tell you. Spare me from any work or effort on my part. Be in my head and be automatically knowing so that I can feel 100 percent secure and loved.

It is as one counselor recently observed: "True love expects you to be a mind reader." This expectation causes an unbelievable amount of static as we try to keep the line of communication open in our marriage. It certainly contributes nothing positive to the need for conscious transmission.

Examples of how symbiosis can be so destructive are innumerable. However, I immediately think of a young couple I will call Kathy and Don. Kathy likes to experiment with new hairstyles. She expects Don to come in from work on days when she has a new one, and automatically exclaim and affirm. They have a good marriage, so she enjoys the luxury of security and stability that can prompt such nonsense. She is not only lulled into presumptuousness by such luxury she also is not courteous enough or wise enough to *say*, "Hi, Honey! How do you like my new hairdo?" She seeks 100 percent affirmation and discovery and she ends up with zero. As a consequence, Kathy spends much of her marriage hurt and unaffirmed.

George comes home, on the other hand, wanting affection and reassurance. He's had a rough time at the office. He's been dumped on, kicked around, and generally unaffirmed. What he wants from his wife is 100 percent affirmation, the kind and amount of affirmation that can possibly offset the discouragement of the day! He does not call her before leaving the office to clue her in. He doesn't transmit his needs clearly as he walks in the door. He needs for her to *know!* After all, if he's got to *ask* for her love and affection, he can get along without it, thank you!

Instead, forgetting to consciously be a transmitter, he walks in the door seeking 100 percent affirmation, all prepared for her to reinstall his self-esteem. Joyce, however, looks at him with bright and pleased eyes and says, "Hi, Honey, would you take out the garbage?" He is hurt, "unloved," "misunderstood," and feels even further put down. And, *it's all his fault!* He has not consciously transmitted his needs. He has assumed she was in his head, that she knew what he needed because "they are just that way." The reality is that true love cannot read minds any more than good secretaries can accurately record garbled messages.

Another example of the unique problems of assumed symbiosis is the man who had an argument with his wife before leaving for work. On his way home from the office that evening he decided to do the mature thing, show his apology and love—and everything would be fine. Rather than wheeling into the garage and walking into the kitchen sniffing under lids on the stove, as was his custom, he stopped in the driveway. He got out of his car, hiding a box of candy and some flowers behind his back, and headed for the front door. There he rang the doorbell and waited patiently. He just knew she would fully understand and appreciate his gesture! Shortly, his wife appeared at the door and immediately burst into tears. After she had regained her composure, she said, "The dishwasher overflowed, my car won't start, Eddie's been a tyrant all day, the goldfish died, Blackie threw up on my new carpet, and now you come home drunk!"

The result was that she was dismayed and he was hurt. The evening and the staged apology were ruined all because he did not *clearly transmit.* He assumed symbiosis and was *expecting* 100 percent affirmation without giving 100 percent clear transmission.

Wise couples learn that true love or sincere intentions cannot read minds or enable mind reading. Wise couples have learned that when they aim at being affirmed by their partner at 100 percent, they usually end up with 5 percent (or minus 5 percent!). The better approach is to try to meet your mate halfway, settle for 50 percent affirmation by being a conscious transmitter. By sending a clear message, thus settling for 50 percent affirmation, you may still end up with only 15 or 20 percent, but 15 or 20 percent is much better than minus 5 percent! And, by meeting your partner halfway, you just could, on occasion, end up with 60 or 70 percent affirmation!

Perhaps the greatest portion of the static on the line of meaningful communication is the assumption that our partner just simply knows what we are thinking or wanting—that because we are so close, we do not need to *tell* them. There are other factors that cause static on the line, that diminish our conscious need to be a clear transmitter, but this assumption of symbiosis is perhaps the greatest.

Too Pooped to Ponder

Another factor the person as transmitter must bear in mind is that some of us are not so presumptuous as we are just plain lazy. We would simply prefer not to do any more than is absolutely necessary to care for and maintain any relationship. We may try to cover our tracks with smug rationalizations like the man who rejected the complaint of his wife that he never told her that he loved her. His response was, "I told you I loved you the day we got married. If I ever change my mind, I'll let you know!" Call it what you may, rationalize as you will, laziness is something the person as conscious transmitter must also bear in mind.

Also, if we are to adequately play our role of being a clear *source* of communication, there is also the need to be aware of the static-causing factor of egocentricity. Some people are information oriented and not communication committed because they simply do not know how, or are not disposed toward being that conscious of *others.* There is no easy cure for this static. A meaningful faith and a lot of hard, personal effort has helped many. Egocentricity does cause static that needs our attention, however, if the husband and wife are to take their appointed turn as transmitter.

There are many things that cause static on the line: Some partners in the marriage are innately just not very caring; some simply do not understand the fundamental need to "get through" as opposed to "give out." They equally fail to appreciate the need to clearly articulate their feelings. Some exhibit variations of the factors already shown. Perhaps many of these shades of previously stated factors can themselves be placed under the overall umbrella of fear of, or inability to be, vulnerable.

Marriage Is a Risky Business

The word *vulnerable* is a very important word and concept to the person in a relationship who is determined to fulfill the important role of being a conscious transmitter. Courageous risk or meaningful vulnerability is imperative if partners in a marriage are to become truly adequate, clear, and concise communicators. The partner, either the husband or wife, in their role as a transmitter has to run the risk of being rejected. They must, of necessity, come to terms with the potential for good or ill that is inherent in exposed and candid feelings. They must deal creatively with self-consciousness, timidity, or native shyness. One must be vulnerable if communication is to be clear, directional, kind, and courteous.

Be a conscious transmitter! Remember that a message that is garbled at the beginning does not clarify itself en route. Tenaciously and tenderly endeavor to inform, to share, and to be vulnerable. As you care for and maintain your good marriage, be conscious of the fact that you are a transmitter. This is at least one-half the job that the persons involved must perform in order to get static off the line. By being conscious that you are a transmitter, communication really becomes a process of common-union. Be determined that you're going to "get through" and not just "give out"!

Receiving Is Harder Than Giving

In communication that is truly common-union both partners must be aware that not only are they transmitters, but if static is to be further cleared from the line, they must also be functioning *receivers*. Clear, concise, and endearing messages require both transmission and reception. Someone has to send the message and someone else must receive that message. Getting through also requires someone near by who can be gotten to!

At times the husband will be the transmitter and at times he will be the receiver. At times the wife will be the transmitter and at times she will be the receiver. The roles must switch back and forth so that the process is mutual. When the process of communication is, in fact and in reality, a mutual undertaking, then static-free common-union can result.

I have to be particularly conscious of this principle in my own marriage. I am actually a better transmitter (I suppose we all are) than I am a receiver. Therefore, I have to work hard not only at sending clear messages but perhaps harder at receiving messages.

I am a rather quiet person around the house, while Sandra is enthusiastic about everything and enjoys talking about whatever interests her. She has had to carry the conversation in the twenty-five-plus years of our marriage. I am only now learning to push myself beyond my laziness and past my early-childhood role models and become more involved in verbal interchange. Now, I am learning what Sandra has always known, that informal talk and simple sharing are important and rewarding to a marriage.

Bad Receiving Can Ruin Good Transmitting

So much communication, our getting through in a marriage, depends on the person who is on the *receiving end*. Many marriages have been hurt and much transmission lost because the second factor was not present. When we as a partner in the marriage are so insecure or defensive that we cannot *hear* and *assimilate*, then even excellent transmission is of no practical use. But, when the receiver is a person who is open to what his or her spouse is trying to transmit, one who is interested and constantly sensitive to subtle undertones, feelings, and implications, then communication has a chance.

An excellent illustration of receiver-as-problem came to my office some time ago in the form of a young lady facing marital problems. She began by saying, "We've got to do something about our miserable sex life!" She then proceeded to tell me what an absolute clod her husband was. He had no sensitivity here, no aptitude there, no softness over yonder, and no gentleness over here! He evidently was a certified failure in bed.

Finally, I interrupted her long enough to ask if she had ever shared any of these feelings with him. She looked at me in shocked annoyance and said, "Certainly not! My husband thinks he's the world's greatest lover and would be absolutely violent if I ever attempted to communicate to him the things I have been telling you. When we *have* to engage in sex, I just fake it and make him think he is just that wonderful."

This could, of course, be a clear case where she was not being a good transmitter, and I had no doubt but that this was part of the problem. But having made that concession, I found myself rather convinced that the real problem was in the reception. Reading the symptoms she shared and following her monologue as objectively as I possibly could, I began to see a man who was so closed, so insecure, and so defensive that *he* had more than likely turned a good transmitter (his wife) into a poor transmitter. Thus, the great fault lay in the receiver. Many people are busy saying, "Why don't you talk to me? Why don't you level with me?" when all the time they are teaching their partner that it isn't safe or creative to do so.

What this story taught me was not only how important receiving was to real communication but also that the receiver could so intimidate the transmitter that they lost their skills also. Static on the line comes from not hearing *and* from throttling the source of communication. Thus, reception—really being receptive—is every bit as important to the process of common-union as is transmission. One without the other is only half the instrumentation required for getting through.

There are, of course, numerous reasons why so many of us are such poor listeners. Perhaps one of the paramount reasons is that listening takes patience. Most people of western civilization are intrinsically not very patient. We not only want what we want *now,* but also what we've got to *say* is so much more important than what is being said that we can hardly wait for the other person to be quiet so we can share our piercing insights. Patience means just what it implies. It means to lie quietly as would a patient and allow someone else to help us. That is fundamentally hard for us. We are basically impatient transmitters who need to remember that patient receptivity, while harder, is equally important.

Why We Listen So Poorly

Some of us are poor receivers not just because it is harder but because we do not understand the fundamental nature of the word *listen*. I think perhaps the essence of this word was more than adequately captured by Dr. Ray Houghton of Berkeley, California, when he penned these words:

> When I ask you to listen to me and you start giving advice, you have not done what I asked.
> When I ask you to listen to me and you begin to tell me why I shouldn't feel that way, you are trampling on my feelings.
> When I ask you to listen to me and you feel you have to do something to solve my problem, you have failed me, strange as that may seem.
> Listen! All I ask is that you listen, not talk, or do . . . just hear.
> Advice is cheap: twenty cents will get you both Dear Abby and Billy Graham in the same newspaper.
> And I can do for myself. I'm not helpless. Maybe discouraged and faltering, but not helpless.
> When you do something for me that I can and need to do for myself, you contribute to my fear and inadequacy.
> But when you accept, as a simple fact, that I do feel, no matter how irrational, then I can quit trying to convince you and get about the business of understanding what's behind this irrational feeling.
> And when that's clear, the answers are obvious and I don't need advice. Irrational feelings make sense when we understand what's behind them.
> So please listen and just hear me. And if you want to talk, wait a minute for your turn, and I'll listen to you.

Hearing is the fundamental nature of the word *listen!* Many people are poor receivers because they have not yet learned to take their turn as a listener so that they can earn their turn as a speaker.

Another reason some of us are poor listeners is that we are not fundamentally interested in the lives, affairs, or feelings of others.

We are so preoccupied with our own lives, affairs, and feelings that the declarations of others come as intrusion or annoyance.

Still others of us are poor listeners because we have not yet learned that the words spoken to us represent but a mere 7 percent of the message intended or the true message being conveyed. Being attuned to the reality that 93 percent of the message is tied to body language, tone of voice, and other nonverbal indicators makes us better listeners in that we begin to "read" and recognize the thought content of expression, nervousness, anxiety, and other thought-saturated expressions.

Cubbyholes and the Big, Wide World

A critical reason why husbands and wives often fail to communicate effectively is that they are not significantly attuned to the fact that men and women think differently. Their minds simply function in different ways. Women, in general, *tend* to be more aesthetic while their counterparts *tend* toward pragmatics. The average woman tends toward more feeling, while most men tend toward a more analytical approach to things. There are, of course, enough obvious exceptions to any rule, and particularly this rule, that I carefully use the word *tend.* They do tend to think in rather predictable and different ways and because they do, real effort must be made by both to take their turn as better listeners.

Paul Unruh, a counselor in Greencastle, Pennsylvania, has helped me to get a little more in practical touch with this difference. He has made the observation that men tend to think in squares while women tend to think in one big circle. Men keep things separated and in nice pat compartments. Women lump everything together in one big bag. Men think in cubbyholes and women take in their whole, wide world.

For instance, a man is quite capable of getting up in the morning, having his breakfast and a cross word with his wife. He puts that moment in its proper box and proceeds to climb into his "driving to work box." Here he tools down the parkway listening to the radio and pretty much leaving the spat at the house in its designated cubbyhole. When he gets to the office, he is in his "office box." When he starts home at the end of the day, he is in his "starting home box." When he gets home, he is perhaps in his "let's have dinner, watch TV, and make love box."

She, on the other hand has spent the whole day with a bad start, no detergent, Aunt Martha's unexpected visit, her office work or club activities, a bad report card, and everything else all wrapped up in *one* bundle. Then, hubby walks through the door with all his tidy little cubicles in his head, ready for new activities as though nothing had happened between them that day, and she cries, "You left home this morning and you didn't kiss me or say you were sorry or . . . !"

She isn't emotional and illogical. He isn't as crass and uncaring as he may seem. They simply think differently! Being aware of this differential can do away with one of the major impediments to receptivity.

In *Two Together* Robert C. Dodds points out the importance of the realization that the husband and wife are not required to think *alike* but to think *together!* Thinking together requires an awareness of difference in approach and temperament.

Yet another reason we often have more difficulty receiving than we do transmitting is that we think we have all the answers and are always right. Anyone who thinks he or she has all the answers and is all-knowing is not only reflecting some persisting inner-child condition but is also greatly disrupting complete communication. People who know all are not open to new points of view. They have a closed mind. They approach communication with an outward show of superiority that is usually founded on inner sources of low self-esteem and insecurity. When either partner bases his or her communication on the premise that there is nothing left to learn or nothing left to say (provided they were the last to speak), then we have a marriage in real trouble. We have real static on the line. There may be great transmission, but there is still very poor reception and therefore no meaningful communication.

There are many reasons why so many of us are better at transmitting than we are at receiving, but suffice it to say, both are necessary for common-union. Both husband and wife must work hard to develop both skills in their relationship. Therefore, couples who cannot or will not speak to each other or who are unable or unwilling to hear each other are very little different from two people sitting in the same canoe. They aren't getting along. They are in conflict and navigational disarray. In order to fix the problem, or settle the matter, they proceed to saw the canoe in half rather than strive for common-union. Both go down when the highest priority is given to "fixing the other" as opposed to fixing the problem.

Let me repeat, even if marriages are made in heaven, the partners involved are required to give it proper care and maintenance. This means work at it. Do it together. Think together! Strive mutually to be better transmitters. Make a conscious effort to be a caring and available receiver. Be both! Be a transmitter and a receiver and be them together for togetherness!

In the next chapter we will look at some guidelines that can help us think together, if not alike.

CHAPTER 10

Communication: Rules for Getting Through

If getting through to our partner in clear communication is an art, then there are rules for developing this art. In fact, there are many such rules. Like a good golf swing, good communication has more rules than the mind can absorb. I often wondered how anyone hit a golf ball right, until I began with the three basic rules: (1) Keep your head down; (2) slow down your back swing; and (3) don't look up to see the beautiful shot *before* you hit the ball. I've found the same help with the glut of rules for clear communication. I have found three that can be labeled as most common, most immediate, and most important. When not followed, they can cause much static on the line; but if observed, they can provide great dividends. Both husband and wife must be willing to: (1) Fight fairly; (2) take the initiative in getting through; and (3) be affirming. There are more rules than these—many more—but these three represent a great beginning.

Rule 1: Fight Fairly

This rule is often overlooked because, for one thing, everyone knows that "nice people" never fight, and good marriages simply do not have conflicts! To speak of such fighting or even of fighting fairly is not only paradoxical but is skating on the thin edge of heresy. The object, so the myth runs, is to find the kind of mate who so blends with our personality and temperament that complete harmony is the result. Once this remarkable confluence occurs—we find the right person and the right person finds us—we are then free to set the cruise control on automatic and lounge in the back of the van enjoying coffee and copulation!

It doesn't work that way. Good marriages are forged! They come by heat and hammer. They come through the *process* of two people working together, thinking together, and expressing a clear willingness to grow up and grow together. *This process* involves some friction and conflict. The primary question, therefore, becomes how shall we handle the inevitable?

One important answer, one practical solution, is to fight fairly! Learn to deal with inevitable problems in such a way that they do not become disruptive static between the transmitter and the receiver.

So common is the problem of normal conflict and the tendency to handle it abnormally, that clinics are beginning to appear here and there across the land that specialize in the fine art of helping couples learn how to fight fairly. Los Angeles has a well-known institution of this type and many more such programs are appearing across the country.

These clinics and individual counselors are attempting to introduce and induce a more healthy approach to normal problem solving. They are attempting to tell us that conflict is not only inevitable but is natural and can be healthy. It is potentially creative if handled properly.

The Apostle Paul himself admonished us, that "we be angry and sin not . . . and not allow the sun to go down on our anger" (*see* Ephesians 4:26). To me, this means that no marriage or faith exists that can or will extricate us from being human. Our "feisty glands" are and *should* be in place though under control, and servant rather than master. To me, Paul's words mean that I should learn how to affirm the value of friction, as a man spinning the wheels of his car on ice can appreciate a handful or two of sand. Paul is encouraging us to learn how to be in control of our energy sources and make them work for us rather than against us and our marriage.

When we hear someone say, "My mom and dad never fought," they may be saying one of two things. Either their mom and dad lived their marriage on a very narrow plane or they had learned the art of fighting fairly (which includes doing it in private). If a couple never experiences conflict or friction, they may simply be committed to living in a state where they are not too glad and not too sad. Or, they may have simply grown so indifferent toward each other that there isn't enough closeness to cause friction. Perhaps they have agreed, either overtly or through default, that theirs will be a marriage of détente. On the other hand, if they are normal and are doing normal things, they may *appear* to be so happily married that they never fight, only because they have learned the fine art of fighting fairly.

Sandra and I have been working on this in our marriage for many years. We feel it has contributed to the fact that the marriage remains both good and growing. We've pretty well worked out the guidelines on this subject on our own. Neither of us have had the opportunity to attend a good clinic on the subject. We have read, communicated, and worked at it and have found the rewards well worth the effort. The insights we have gained we would like to share with you.

Avoid Hidden Agenda

Perhaps the cardinal rule in fighting fairly is knowing full well *what the fight is all about!* Too often disruptive static is created by either the husband or the wife because they are not dealing squarely and honestly with the issue at hand. They are bringing to the present conflict old or unsettled conflicts with a parent way back in childhood. They perceive their spouse as "treating me just like my mom did." We didn't like it then and never won in that conflict, so now we use a relatively insignificant problem in our marriage as a pretext for rehashing old grievances. The little boy or girl still within us, still in conflict with mom or dad or other family interactions, is the source of much of the hidden agenda within our marital conflicts.

Hidden agenda may come from this source or from any number of sources. For instance, we may come home from the office feeling battered and abused. Our mate commits a trivial trespass and we blow it all out of proportion. We don't understand why we are so angry, and our spouse does not understand why we are so angry. The reason is hidden agenda (in the form of office abuse) in search of a scapegoat. The problem, our spouse's trivial trespass, is not really that big. If we would concentrate on the trespass and not use it as the occasion to vent other frustrations or hostilities, we could fight more fairly.

Fighting fairly means that we do not allow the loss of an expected promotion, or any extraneous frustration, to become a reason to yell at our spouse or kick the dog!

It is imperative that we fight fairly—that we deal with the issue confronting us and not add to it through hidden agenda of superfluous baggage. We must recognize that creating a conflict over a cup of lukewarm coffee will not compensate for the threat of middle age. Attacking a husband for not balancing the checkbook does not correct low self-esteem. Making mountains out of molehills will not create smooth travel to a mutual goal. Through awareness and effort we fight more fairly by minimizing the influence and impact of hidden agenda. In my own life, I have found the best tip-off that hidden agenda is gumming up communication is feeling excessively angry over something not *that* significant. I ask myself, why am I *so* angry over this? I usually discover that I'm bringing a load of disappointment or resentment from somewhere *else* and dumping it on this petty issue to vent *all* my hostile feelings. I also discover in my marriage, and in the marriage of others, a tendency to do this dumping on the person who loves me the most. I presume on their love, place pressure on our love—all because I do not choose to fight fairly, I must learn to fight fairly!

Explore—Don't Exploit—the Past

This second point flows logically from the first. As we saw in chapter two, we do carry around within ourselves every little boy or girl we ever were. One of the important applications of this awareness is not letting that little child garble communication in our marriage.

For instance, the statement "Don't treat me like a child" usually indicates past and persisting agenda that someone once did. Recognize the fact that someone once treated you childishly—habitually and annoyingly—and that your spouse may be so close to that old ground that they are now triggering those old tapes. Explore this with your mate. Work together on the *now*. Do not allow yourself to exploit the past by continuing to be a victim when you really need to grow up and become a mature partner in a relationship. Do not allow your partner to exploit either your past or theirs by charging or blundering into sensitive areas where old scars remain. In short, do not allow the past to be used as either shield or club.

I was out jogging one hot summer afternoon. The sun was bright, the temperature was in the mid-nineties, and the humidity had to have been about as high as the heat. About half-way around a lovely jogging trail, I paused on the edge of a lake on the campus of the University of Florida to take a badly needed break. As I sat on a cypress log panting and wanting to die, a car stopped on the adjacent road. A man jumped out, came over to me, and said, "I need to talk to you about my marriage!" My first thought was to throw him into the lake with the alligators. I smiled instead and said, "What's the problem?" For the next forty-five minutes he poured out his problems while I baked in the sun and filled my shoes with cascading perspiration. What he said in those forty-five minutes was, in effect: "My marriage is getting into a mess and it's my fault! I keep accusing my wife of being unfaithful and she isn't and I know she isn't! I'm wondering," he continued, "could my mistrust be coming from hearing my dad say over and over that all women were tramps?" I said, "Could it?" He said, "Yes, it could." He then ended my hour of relaxation and freedom by walking away mumbling something about his need to keep his dad's paranoia out of his own marriage!

Fighting fairly will also help you get static off the lines of communication. Explore your past for insights and perspective, but do not allow your past to exploit you!

Don't Yell at Each Other Unless . . .

Many times we increase our volume to compensate for lack of clarity or strength of position. But yelling only adds static to the static that is already on the line. It does not clear up anything. It does not shore up a weak position. It only adds to the problem.

I've noticed in my own marital conflicts the same truth I have discovered in hundreds of other marriages—the more I increase my volume the weaker I know my argument really is. The louder we yell the more unsure of ourselves and our position we really are. Not only that, we also add to the confusion, hurt, and poor communication.

Yet another problem with yelling is that it uses up much needed energy. With sensitivity, control, and conservation we could use that same energy to improve our relationship.

The same is true of energy spent in defensiveness. If a lot of yelling is going on, the other partner is required by circumstances, if not by their nature, to expend an inordinate amount of energy just to keep from being blown over. Just yesterday a lady sat in my office and said, "I'm getting a divorce because of sheer exhaustion. I can no longer stand the abuse." I asked her if her husband beat her. "No," she said. "When we have a problem, he yells until he won't speak again for a week, and as for me, I've tried for eighteen years to stand upright in this wind tunnel, until I no longer possess the will to stand. I'm getting out!" How sad and how unnecessary! We all have such good energy in store to help us face the tasks we must face. If we'd just use it where it would do some good, we would be so much happier.

Don't yell at each other unless the house is on fire!

Avoid the Words Never *and* Always!

If I were teaching in one of the "fight fairly" clinics, this would be my fourth point. Be careful about using words or statements that perpetuate the crisis by painting your partner into a corner.

One of the prevailing difficulties in learning to fight fairly is the compulsion to zap the other with such zingers as, "You *always* act like a two-year-old when I express an opinion that is different from yours!" We like to say, "You *never* do the things around the house you promise you'll do!"

Always and *never* tend to create always and never! Such negative suggestions are lethal because they paint us into corners from which we might escape were we given encouragement and incentive.

Negative suggestion plays a disruptive part in all of life. It is a factor that must be reckoned with in fair fighting. For instance, often a parent will say, "Now Junior, you always disobey me and do just what I tell you not to do. Don't walk through that mud puddle!" Junior obliges and goes tromp, tromp right through the middle! The parent usually assumes they have inherited a young Frankenstein when in reality they are actually programming Junior through negative suggestion. Verbally or nonverbally they have painted him into a corner that may be as uncomfortable for him as it is for them.

A young lady came up to me in Burbank, California, one day. She said, "I don't really enjoy the teen drug scene. I'd like to stay away from it but my mother so suspects me of it, I feel drawn toward it!" Exactly! It's called negative suggestion because it is autosuggestion via negative absolutes.

It's the mother who leaves home and says, "Junior! Mommie's going to be gone for a few minutes, don't poke peas up your nose!" He does, and she simply does not understand. She simply does not understand that negative suggestions breed negative conduct.

This situation also exists between partners in a marriage. Many a destructive or annoying habit has been perpetuated in a marriage because "you always" and "you never" program the partner toward fulfilling the expectations that are laid out for them.

When a wife says, "You *never* act the way I want you to when we visit my family," she is setting a stage of continuity. When she says, "You *always* forget to take out the garbage," she is as delinquent as he. When he says, "You *never* listen to me when I'm trying to explain something" or "You *always* give the kids more attention than you do me," he is effectively painting her into a corner that is uncomfortable for both.

Fighting fairly also means never say never and always avoid always. This rule can help eliminate static on the line.

Don't Bite Off More Than You Can Eschew!

Don't say things from which there is no escape later. This would be the fifth guideline I would share in any course on how to fight fairly. Do not invoke irrevocable truths. Don't say things that are true, but irrelevant, that you may need to escape from later!

The scenario usually goes something like this. George has found a new toy he wants, and new toys for people George's age are usually quite expensive. He gently approaches Judy, his wife, and sets her up. He introduces this new item that will bring total fulfillment to his life. She knows she is on the spot. She knows she needs to respond as nonthreateningly as possible and finally says, "But, George dear, we can't afford that right now."

George knew in his heart pretty much what she would say and

that she was right. But he wanted this new toy because it would, in his fantasy, bring complete meaning to his life. So now he launches his all-out attack. He responds to her true statement by saying, "Oh yeah! Well, well, well . . . you've got a double chin!" Now, if she *has* a double chin, he can certainly win the battle (the battle no longer being the toy but his need to punish her for her refusal) with such a statement but has also sealed his own fate as to the outcome of the war.

He has now invoked an irrevocable truth, and *years* later she will say, "You said I had a double chin!" "I didn't mean it!" he will exclaim, but having bitten off more than he can shun or shed, he has initiated some degree of static on the line for perhaps a long, long time.

It is amazing what people will say when not guarding against fighting dirty! And, it is equally amazing what they sacrifice in the future in order to win a quick victory in the present. If we are negotiating a new car, sex, or a new wardrobe with our mate, and they are negative toward the idea, we dare not "win" the argument by saying "You've got fat thighs!" Such a statement is irrelevant to the subject even if it's true. It is unkind even if it is true. It is also unbelievably static causing, especially if it is true! And, because it is true, it is a statement from which you can never escape.

Truths such as skinny legs, crooked nose, overbite, impotency, and a bossy mother are superfluous and destructive to any subject other than legs, noses, teeth, impotency, and in-law relationships. The more *accurate* and irrelevant the statement is the more lingering and disruptive it will become.

Don't introduce something that you will need or want to shun, shed, or disclaim at a later date. Punishing your spouse now punishes you *and* them further on down the line. If you would fight fairly and help keep static off the line, don't say things you will not want to live with later.

Rule 2: Take the Initiative

If rule number one in clearing static on the line is fighting fairly, then rule number two is not waiting for someone else to clear it up. You take the initiative. It is generally easier to wait for the other person to say, "I'm sorry" or "Let's talk about it," but your saying it *first* often leads to both of you eventually saying it simultaneously.

This second rule is so general and all-encompassing that it is applicable to the healing or correcting of virtually any problem within a marriage. I'll discuss it in its more general application in the next chapter but deal with it here only as it applies to clarity of communication.

If it is true, as I have previously alleged, that everyone is hard to live with and that the only real difference is that some people give us enough in return to make the effort worthwhile, then all of us have faults. It is precisely as Sloan Wilson writes in *A Summer Place:* "It's not a question of who's going to throw the first stone; it's a question of who's going to start building with it." We must strive to be the *first* to build with the stone we could just as easily, and perhaps justifiably, throw. Being helpful tends to generate helpfulness. Taking the initiative clears the way for mutual initiative. This is a rule for getting static off the important lines of communication.

Some marriage partners exclaim, "It's just not fair!" In this exclamation there is an implication. The implication is, why should *I* carry the bigger load when *my spouse* is the real culprit? I want static off the line but not at that expense!

In an effort to help get static off the line, let me point out a truth so obvious that it is constantly overlooked. If he or she is *in fact* the more guilty, the more childish, or the more unhealthy, then the healthier, more wholesome person in *the relationship*—in any relationship—has to carry the bulk of the burden! If I am a cripple, emotionally or physically, and you are stable and strong, then bear me up in love until I can gain my footing and my health! If I am healthy and the more stable at this time, then I will move *first* to avoid conflict or to correct communication.

Taking the initiative will generally produce more favorable results than waiting for 100 percent affirmation *or* 100 percent surrender from your partner. If your wife is in her period, mad at the world, and not handling it or you very well, go help her in the kitchen! Take the initiative *especially* if you are the innocent one, by reason of being the healthier and better adjusted.

It is nice when both partners in the relationship can carry an equal amount of the load in the marriage, but this is seldom the case at any given time. During one day or decade, he leans on her. On another day or decade, she leans on him. One good turn not only deserves another but also sets the pattern for the switch in roles that appears to be inevitable in marriages that cover many years of togetherness. To be able to talk about these role changes and the logic of healthy maneuverability through *clear,* static-free communication is greatly aided and abetted by sensible initiative. This healthy initiative can be an investment that may return great dividends to the marriage.

Rule 3: Be Affirming

While rule three is an important key to keeping a good thing going (as we will see in chapter eleven) it is equally important in static-free communication.

There is a simple reason why this rule is a static-clearing rule. It is important to the subject of this chapter because it is infinitely easier to speak clearly, lovingly, and without hidden agenda or extraneous baggage to a person who *loves* you and *shows* you that love. If your spouse is affirming to you, you in turn can be more loving. If we, again taking the initiative, are truly affirming of them, they receive both incentive and enablement. Love generates being loving and being loving gets a lot of static off the line!

Working at being affirming is to strive to help our partner not only recognize our love but feel better about *themselves.* When we all feel better about ourselves, we, in turn, tend toward reciprocation in kind. This approach seldom works over the long haul when utilized as a gimmick or as a ploy, but when it is a conscious expression of our life-style, it can lead to many clear understandings and mutual affirmations. As someone has observed, what is needed in our sex life today (as well as in all forms of intimate interaction) is not *technique* but *tenderness!* What is needed in *all* of our marital endeavors is not so much skill but caring. Not power that overwhelms and conquers but love that engenders loving.

When we consciously work to help our partner feel better about themselves, we have gone far in removing static from the line. It *is* a great principle and vital rule. We *must* make a deliberate choice to live affirmingly with our partner if we want to reduce static on the line. This task is not necessarily an easy task. Some of us will have to fight that inner child of the past. Others will have to struggle with immaturities or insecurities that prevent our living affirmingly. But, affirm our partner we must. Without affirmation, communication can be lost in heavy static. With affirmation we all discover how much easier it is to share candidly with someone who loves us and supports us. As one man said recently, "I have learned that 'I love you. I am on your side' is worth two hours of debate."

Clear communication requires a transmitter and a receiver. In the case of marriage, this is one spouse endeavoring to get through to another spouse who is equally willing to be *gotten to*. These two *partners* constitute the most important part of communication. Three of the most important guidelines for helping them get through are to fight fairly, take the initiative, and be affirming.

CHAPTER 11

Keys to Keeping a Good Thing Going

Essentially, this book has concentrated on the *unique* problems to be found in *good* marriages and why even good marriages require care and maintenance. What has been said can and does apply to bad marriages, but it is important to remember that most bad marriages are good marriages *gone* bad! This important point keeps our primary focus on the question, how do I keep a good thing good? If a good marriage is not automatic and self-perpetuating, what can be done to give it proper care and meaningful maintenance? In this final chapter we list some practical keys for keeping a good marriage going. The list is not exhaustive, but features the ones I consider most necessary.

Key 1: Keep on Dating

Hands down, this first key is number one because it *is* first and primary! Everything else that can be said, and will be said, is basically elaboration and exploration of this fundamental point. To keep on dating *after* the wedding is so critical, so imperative, that it probably constitutes the major reason for silver and golden anniversaries.

The more you and your mate can *continue* the approach, the attitudes, and the expressions of your courtship, the happier and more stable the marriage will be. These were the actions and interactions that caused you to fall in love! These remain the actions and interactions that sustain your love for each other.

The tragedy is that many or most couples discontinue dating habits and expressions once they are securely married. They carelessly lay aside the very attributes that attracted the one to the other. As I see such couples in my office, dozens upon dozens of them, I often say to myself, "Here are two nice people, hurting people, who started out with so much hope but *left their brains at the altar.*" They stopped thinking and with that he or she began leaving out the very courtesies and endearing expressions that caused them to fall in love in the first place. When this process begins, the usual result is not *just* the discontinuing of the loving, thinking, thoughtful actions of courtship *but* also an automatic lapse into a subconscious reproduction of one's early home life.

He stops thinking and, therefore, dating and begins to treat her the way he saw his dad treat his mother. She stops thinking, planning, and programming his affections and feelings and slides into the patterns she knew in childhood. When we use our mind, we can be our best self. When we feel securely married and stop using our mind, we tend simply to reproduce our early role models. Soon, you hear her say, "You're not the man I married!" He says, "You're just like your mother!" Both are probably right, but the problem lies in the fact that they did not keep on dating after saying, "I do!"

In fact, the tendency to stop dating seems to be one of the unique problems of truly good marriages. In a weak or insecure marriage one or both partners may keep some dating mentality out of self-defense, insecurity, or a subconscious awareness that things are not safe enough to stop. For example, if you marry someone whom you know to be immature or to have tendencies toward unfaithfulness, you are much more apt to keep on thinking, working at it, winning, and wooing. It is when we marry someone who is stable, solid, and deeply in love with us that we tend to become lazy. We put our brain in neutral and slip back to the old familiar patterns we grew up with.

Positively, I would state the key in this way: Treat your partner *after* marriage in the same way you did when you were trying to win and secure his or her love! Keep thinking. Keep working. Keep on dating!

The subtleness of this point could bear some further exploration. It is not hard to perceive in principle but often escapes us in practical expression. Having stated the key, let's look at the problem a little more closely.

Before marriage, the young man will open the door of the car for his girl friend. This act is important to their budding relationship because it demonstrates his affection, respect, and affirmation. After marriage, however, when she is tired, or pregnant, or not feeling well and may actually need the help, he tends to discontinue this expression of esteem and affirmation.

Before marriage both parties attempt to dress in such a way as to affirm and attract the other. After marriage there is a tendency to let down in this area. There is, of course, a legitimate need to have a place called home where one can be more at ease, but being more at ease should not allow us to slip into an attitude that nonverbally communicates to our partner that he or she is less important.

Many of our once-good marriages are just that, once-good marriages, because they have discarded something so simple as affirming appearance within the home. A young man who came to my office some years ago stated the problem in his marriage rather eloquently. He said, "The first thing that went in our marriage was her underwear. When I walked into our bedroom night after night and saw her standing there with a rubber band around her waist and a few shreds of dacron and cotton hanging here and there, I knew we were in trouble!" Even if he was overstating the case, he was at least verbalizing *his* impression of it.

She, of course, is putting a finger on the same problem when *she* must complain incessantly about his unshaven face on weekends. She does not enjoy being "told" that everyone down at the office is important and that she can be taken for granted.

They are both saying what was captured in a recent cartoon. It pictured two grubby people watching TV. He had a beer can sitting on his big stomach, was unshaven, and sloppy in general. She was dressed in a bathrobe two sizes too large, curlers in her hair, and saying, "What happened? Where is the rush, the magnetism, the magic we once knew?" He responds, "I think it all started when you stopped putting on makeup."

She could just as easily say, "When you started burping without apology." "When you started picking your teeth with your steak knife." "When you stopped doing the things you once did and when you started doing things you *never* did!" All point to the same positive need—keep on *doing* the things that made me love you and keep on *not* doing the things that distract from our love.

Another expression of the problem constantly turns up in sex in general and foreplay specifically. While I am personally of the "old school" of waiting until the marriage, I nevertheless am compelled to work with the destructive "new school" of "do it if it feels good." When I am placed in the role of listening to the consequences of this "new" undisciplined, indulgent life-style, I remind myself that I am a counselor at this moment and not a preacher of the moment. If I am to help, I must be a helper and not a judge. When I get down to the business of helping, I usually uncover yet another expression of the problem. The story seldom varies.

I am often told by college students and other singles that "things were just great before we got married!" They go on to tell me that after marriage everything changed. A little digging into the relationship soon reveals that with many of them, before marriage and before sex, foreplay went on for hours! Before marriage, the couples having sex would engage in mutual foreplay and fondling until their eyes were glassy and steam was coming out of their ears! (Interestingly enough, this is even more true of "Christian couples," who often engage in "brinkmanship.") After marriage this "dating" technique is one of many that is often abruptly laid aside. Long periods of holding, touching, and preparing are more often than not replaced with jump in bed, do the expected thing, and get on with something else.

My point is not a defense of the permissive life-style. Quite the contrary, I find that the more undisciplined sex participated in by an engaged couple the more difficult are marital adjustments (*see* diagrams on page 94). This is the very important point I am trying to make: *Dating* before marriage (however that term may be individually translated) and *non*dating after marriage is *lethal!* A couple, straights *or* swingers, must keep *dating*. The rule does not change simply because one couple are the good guys in the white hats and another couple wears black (by the standards I hold).

All married couples, regardless of philosophy or world view, must keep on dating. And, there are some critical test questions for us to contemplate.

Ask Three Essential Questions

The philosophy of "keep on dating" requires every married couple to ask three essential questions. These questions go to the heart of what it means to maintain a courtship philosophy in marriage. The first question asks, "How would I *act?*"

If your partner were not legally bound to you, you know you would not allow yourself to act like the two-year-old you can resemble at times. You would not be the blatant chauvinist you can become. You would not act like an irresponsible fool. You would not be so inconsiderate. You would not . . . The list is endless! First, raise the question how would I *act* if we were not married and still dating? After asking this critical question, begin *acting* like that at the moment.

Second, ask yourself, "How would I *look?*" When you are trying to win someone, you dress winsomely! You dress to look in a way that is calculated to keep your partner looking. You dress to attract and to be attractive. You are saluting yourself and your partner. This process helps get two people together, and it is equally important in helping them stay together! When attempting to keep a courtship mentality warm and glowing in marriage, the second question is, "How would I *look* if my partner were not legally bound to me?"

The third question you must ask is, "How would I *listen?*" If you were not married, how would you listen to what she/he is now saying? How *did* you listen to your partner during your courtship days? You know the answer! Then, you would listen with objectivity, using conscious control, scrupulously avoiding defensiveness, and trying very hard to be vulnerable. You would listen affirmingly to win your partner; you must continue listening affirmingly to keep them. In order to stay together you will want to act, look, and listen in the same ways that got you together. Therefore, keep a dating mentality!

Work At It!

This first key—keep on dating—requires a great deal of effort. The entire concept was summarized in a remark made to me by a gentleman I met in Orlando, Florida, some months ago. We had just met and he was telling me that he and his wife were celebrating their fiftieth wedding anniversary that day. I am always interested in that kind of achievement and generally ask the same sincere question: "What's the secret?"

Without hesitation he said, "Don't take each other for granted and work at it!"

That's what I am trying to say! Work at it! Keep on dating! The dating mentality cultivates the social personality we discussed in chapter three. Our social personality is what we really want to *be*. It cultivates the steps we want to take beyond our natural personality, the person we are when we *do not think* and *are not working at* being a better social companion. Continuous dating demands that we do not leave our brain out of the relationship and just do what comes naturally from our early role models. It mandates that we continue being a thinking, sensitive partner in the marriage.

The first, and perhaps the most important key is keep on dating! Keep asking how would I act, look, and listen if we were not securely married? Then, *do it* now just as you did it then!

Key 2: Be Loyal

Loyalty is a many-faceted word. Perhaps the most common aspect of the word has to do with sexual fidelity. *Fidelity*, which Webster calls "strict adherence to the marriage vow," is critical to the care and maintenance of a good marriage. It is critical because loyalty and trustworthiness is the foundation on which everything good and substantial in the relationship must be built. And, it is critical because being loyal to one person is more fun than being disloyal ever was, and all marriages need fun! When fun and trust leave a relationship, very little, perhaps nothing, is left on which to build.

Phillips Brooks, a famous preacher of a bygone day, put this great truth this way: "Keep clear of concealment, keep clear of the need of concealment. It is an awful hour when the first necessity of hiding anything comes. The whole life is different thenceforth. When there are questions to be feared and eyes to be avoided and subjects which must not be touched, then the bloom of life is gone."

In over twenty years of working with married couples I have found Brooks' statement all too true. When concealment becomes necessary and hiding anything is a way of life, the bloom of life is gone! Loyalty, understood as marital fidelity, is the firm foundation on which any great house must be built.

Important as sexual fidelity may be, it is equally important that this word *loyalty* be *expanded* to encompass a much broader dimension. I, therefore, wish to use the word as it appears in this second key to mean primarily *total loyalty* to my life's partner *in any and all areas.* This concept *includes* sexual fidelity but goes beyond it.

By "going beyond" I do not mean that I can become so loyal that I never again find another person attractive. Nor, does it suggest I will obtain such a state of grace I will never again let my wife down. "Going beyond" does mean, however, that I can become so all-encompassingly loyal that I can enjoy a masterpiece in a museum—or on a street corner—without having to take it home! It means if I do let my partner down somewhere, *I* in turn will be loyal enough to keep on working at loyalty. I would never quit trying to be *totally* faithful in all things, and I would strive for total loyalty as consistently as is humanly possible.

Be Supportive in All Ways

This broader interpretation of loyalty means, for instance, do not disparage your spouse in front of the children. It means that we must be careful not to raise an eyebrow at junior when dad makes a mistake. It means not exchanging knowing glances with a daughter when her mother is expressing herself. It means not talking about our spouse behind his or her back to fellow employees or friends.

Loyalty is being supportive always in all ways. It means telling your partner if something they do or say is disruptive to your life but *not telling anyone else!*

Being loyal may also mean taking our partner back when they have gone astray. Some of the best marriages I know are cases where one strayed and the other forgave. That's loyalty! That's "for better or worse . . . in sickness, or in health . . . for as long as ye both shall live"! This is not just the process of intelligent people remembering that it *usually* takes the failure of *both* partners to cause infidelity, it is also the process of coming to a realization of what is meant by total loyalty. Total loyalty means I will stand by you, you stand by me, and we'll see this life through together!

Total loyalty also means being loyal to oneself. The idea may sound contradictory but it is not. "Two become one" occurs *best* when people in the marriage are equals. Both have to feel unique, special, and know that they are giving up personal rights. When one person in the relationship is disloyal to self by becoming a doormat, constantly going along to get along or surrendering all his or her own rights, the two never really become one.

Being loyal to self and to each other is of vital importance! Loyalty has dimensions *and* potential that are the making or the breaking of a good marriage. I like the way Ruth Stafford Peale captured this principle in an article in the *Christian Herald.* She says: "Marriage must meet the needs of three elemental emotional hungers: (1) I need to feel that *I* march at the head of my wife or husband's parade. That *my* happiness and welfare comes first with my spouse. (2) Everyone needs somebody else's strength. Life is full of awkward burdens; no one should have to carry them all alone or feel that they are being neglected by their special partner. (3) Everyone needs to be needed!"

Loyalty is a critical key to keeping a good marriage going. It means supporting your partner in his or her uncertainties. It means to help your partner during stumblings, hoping he or she will do the same for you when your time comes. It means affirming your partner in those moments when he or she reaches out for help. It means uncompromising loyalty to your partner's hopes, dreams, and need for self-esteem. All this is not only good and right; it is vital. Faithfulness to your partner in *all* things is the greatest of all investments in your *own* hopes and dreams.

Be loyal!

Key 3: Concentrate on the Present and Future

This third key does not contradict earlier statements on the need to explore our past (*see* chapter two). But this key does encourage us to *concentrate* on the now. We must all know where we've *been,* but in the care and maintenance of a good marriage it is even more important to know where we *are* and where we are *going.* If we spend all our time trying to relive the positive past *or* grave digging in the mistakes of the past, all the great possibilities of the present and especially the future can be forfeited.

It is sometimes difficult for couples truly in love to better manage the good old days. We hear many of these couples asking, "Why can't we go back to the way we were?" But, as one commentator said, "All the pounding on the doors of time can't bring back one second of past intimacy! Unless companions live *together* in the *now,* they cannot live together at all."

This reference is obviously to the good things of the past—the way "it used to be when we were dating," or to times of less strife or better days. But the insight must be applied to harboring and haranguing past failures or mistakes. "Twelve years ago you did such and such" is never an adequate substitute for "what have we learned from our mistakes, and what do we do now, and where do we go from here."

I would simply add these words: Adjust or bust! Accept, forgive, forget, affirm, or bury the past, but live in the NOW and look for a better tomorrow!

All couples need to realize that the past *is* behind and that they must learn to concentrate on the present. Every couple needs to work hard on giving the present and the future all they have—living in it, enjoying it, and making the most of it. Don't let the past turn into an anchor that holds you back. Use the past—its painful experiences *and* good memories—as a motivation to make the most out of the present and the future.

Key three is let your *primary concentration* be on the present and on the future.

Key 4: Accentuate the Positive

Every marriage has positive and negative factors. The question therefore becomes which of the two options will become the primary focus of your marriage? Will you accentuate the negative or the positive?

The choice is yours and in making this choice you become part of the process of creating more of what you have chosen. If you look at the negative side of things, not only will you see more of the negative, but more negative acts will *create* more negative acts through your attitude and approach. If you seek to accentuate the positive side of things, you will see more positive things, and more positive aspects are apt to emerge within the relationship. Couples tend to give each other precisely what each partner looks for and expects to receive. Therefore, a very important key to keeping a good marriage going is to accentuate the positive!

Accentuating the positive is a very practical key to maintaining a good marriage because through it we all find what we are looking for. There is a story about two birds flying over the California desert. One is a vulture and the other is a hummingbird. The vulture looks for death and rot. The hummingbird looks for the small nectar-laden flowers in the cactus plant. Both find what they are looking for! When applied to human beings, the analogy becomes even more powerful. In the case of personal human interaction we all help generate what we find! Vultures and hummingbirds can't do that! Birds can only discover what is there. Human beings can *create* what is there by looking for the positive side of things.

Put another way, most counselors accept the principle that I cannot change the way someone acts toward me. Other people direct their own mind, their own will, and their own determinations. The *best* I can do is change the way *I* act *toward them*. If *I* change, especially toward the positive, then my partner has the incentive and opportunity to change also. Since positive breeds positive, it is a practical, workable key for caring for and maintaining a good marriage.

For example, a young man came to my office recently complaining that his wife was driving him up the wall with possessiveness. She was going through a period of deep insecurity and clung to him desperately. He saw her insecurity in a purely negative light and responded with anger and resentment. Naturally this only increased her insecurity and her desperation.

I encouraged him to think about the situation in a more positive light. I suggested that he realize and appreciate his position as the single most important person in his wife's life. When she was clinging to him in fright and insecurity, she, in fact, was turning for support and understanding to the one person whom she trusted and loved most in the entire world. While he did not want to be swallowed up by her desperation, he did need to realize his importance to her. While he did not want to encourage her dependence, he *did need* to appreciate the positive side of the situation—the unique compliment he was receiving. He brightened up and while he made no comment, the smile on his face and the square of his shoulder told me he had discovered a new idea—accentuate the positive!

I learned later that he had practiced precisely what he had discovered and, in so doing, had made yet another discovery. He found, as many do, that looking on the positive side of things not only helps you find what you are looking for but also helps *create* what you are looking for! She began to be more positive because, in changing *his* approach, he had helped her feel so much more secure.

Accentuating the positive is helpful, for instance, when a husband has trouble with the fact that his wife is beginning to appear older. It is this negative awareness that prompts such comments as, "I don't mind my wife being married to a grandfather but I don't like being married to a grandmother!"

As in all things, however, there is a positive side, a beautiful side to this aging process if we will just *look* for it! Marty Robbins commented beautifully on this positive side when he wrote: "Hands that are strong but wrinkled, doing work that never gets done. Hair that's lost some of the beauty by too many hours in the sun. Eyes that show some disappointment, and there's been quite a lot in her life. But she's the foundation I lean on, my woman, my woman, my wife."* What beauty there is in growing more beautiful together. That marvelous positive side is there if you'll just look for it just beneath the wrinkles.

Three Ways to Be Positive

A positive approach to marriage asks three basic questions: (1) what do I really want from marriage? (2) what am *I* doing to endanger my marriage? and, (3) what can *I* do about it?

Perhaps the answer to all three of these questions is the same answer that gets us in touch with how to accentuate the positive. That answer is *practice being an affirming person.* Work at helping your partner feel better about who he or she is.

This, like many "answers," is easier said than done. Being an affirming person requires being a vulnerable person, and for so many people being *vulnerable* is one of the most difficult tasks within marriage. Being vulnerable means sticking your neck out, running some risks, taking the chance of being rejected or laughed at. Don't protect yourself; instead, try to make your partner feel better. Your marriage will win! Take your armor off and be vulnerable. Vulnerability is what each partner needs in order to be affirming of the other partner!

But, being affirming and accentuating the positive is difficult. Husbands and wives are often hesitant to take off the armor because

---

* Copyright © 1969 by Mariposa Music, Inc. Used by permission.

they have never *seen* it done! They never once saw mom and dad being vulnerable or affirming or positive. They now would like to be vulnerable in their own marriage but have never been shown how. They have feelings of self-consciousness combined with ingrained behavioral habits that make the task of showing positive affirmation through vulnerability extremely difficult.

Because of early-childhood negative orientations many marriage partners actually prefer the negative. They hold this strange preference not because they enjoy living in such a way but because they are used to it! Familiarity breeds contentment. As Marshall McLuhan points out, many people prefer bad news to good news because good news requires change and bad news simply requires a survival instinct. Accentuating the positive demands a change in many people. They may try to do so. They may wander a short distance into a more positive, loving life-style but then, sensing they are on unfamiliar ground, retreat to what may be the norm for them—old, familiar negative interaction.

This kind of panic is typical of the people who can handle a good job or a good marriage for just so long and then submit to a compulsion to break and run. Their excuse for breaking and running usually is "I like a challenge!" They say they enjoy doing something until they get on top, but then they want greater challenges. This is what they *say!* For some of us it is true enough that we do enjoy new challenges. But, the larger truth is often the fact that we cannot handle the greatest challenge in all the world—that of keeping a *good* thing going! We may actually be running away *because* we can't handle real challenge. It is easier for anyone to rebuild from scratch than to maintain by scratching. Only the *truly brave* will resist destroying or deserting the truly good job or marriage simply because they cannot bear the thought of losing it. Be positive about what you have acquired and keep on scratching.

Without question, to be positive, to be vulnerable, and to be affirming is difficult for many within many marriages. But the choice is yours and the need to be so still remains.

Be positive through the kind of vulnerability that allows you to be affirming. In every marriage, you find what you are looking for and you help generate what you want in the relationship. Accentuate the positive and you may find you have accelerated the positive!

Key 5: Cultivate a Sense of Humor

It has been suggested that when people are confronted with stress, they are basically still jungle animals with two earthly instincts: fight or flight. There is a third possibility—laugh! While you are disciplining yourself to *learn* to see the positive side of your marriage and your partner within the marriage, discipline yourself with equal tenacity to learn how to find the humorous side. Take your marriage seriously, *not yourself*.

Obviously the role models you had while growing up will affect your ability to laugh or treat some heavy things lightly. But, even if we have never seen how it is done, we can still *cultivate* a redeeming sense of humor. Such a marvelous quality can either be a master-stroke of luck *or* a masterly striving for an indispensable key to keeping a good thing going. Learn to laugh!

Martin Buxbaum tells of two women overheard discussing marriage at a party. One of the women said, "My husband and I have managed to be happy together for twenty years. I guess this is because we're both in love with the same man."* Her redeeming sense of humor enabled her to accept her rather typical husband and laugh about typical idiosyncrasies. It is this grace or gift or gain that *enables* couples to arrive at twenty-year anniversaries. We find that humor is another way of accentuating the positive and increasing our love.

A good, healthy sense of humor is important to *everything* that is demanding. For instance, Hugh Missildine says, "When we think of cruelly oppressed ethnic groups we are likely to attribute their survival to the different cultural strengths—the fight of the Irish, the genius of the Jews, the long-suffering good nature of the blacks, etc." We do. These stereotypes are simplistic and questionable, but many are accepted as fact and much survival is attributed to their reality. But Missildine also points out that these highly generalized ethnic assumptions may not be accurate and may not be the real reason hard-pressed ethnic groups have been able to survive and prosper. He points out that more times than not, their survival is predicated on "a developed sense of humor."

Notice, for instance, how many stand-up comics, comedians, and other humorous entertainers come from minorities and from tough neighborhoods. Any roll call of these entertainers leaves you im-

---

* Reprinted with permission from the January 1982 *Reader's Digest*.

pressed with the fact that perhaps 75 percent of them come from
Brooklyn or The Bronx or some other area that presented a
greater-than-average challenge to survival!

Perhaps the message from all this is not that humorous people
move to tough worlds but that tough worlds produce a need to cultivate a sense of humor.

Marriage is a tough world! Its demand for maturity, its incessant
appetite for growth, and its mandate for compromise, vulnerability,
and togetherness make it so demanding that few couples make it
through who do not learn to laugh at each other and with each
other.

A person who has not inherited this marvelous trait, a sense of
humor, will have to work toward developing it. They will have to
think, study, try, practice, watch, and then, do it all again! It won't
be easy but it is necessary.

The partner who has the trait by nature will need to keep it active
and growing. If we can look for the positive and find it, we can also
look for the humorous and avoid much flight and fight!

Key 6: Take the Initiative

I mentioned this key as a tip for better communication back in
chapter ten, but taking the initiative has a much broader application as it reaches to all aspects of marriage. I find in many couples
that the person who is most capable of taking the initiative is
usually the one who doesn't think it is quite fair that they should
take the initiative in healing a given situation. They say, "I haven't
caused this mess! *They* are the one with the drinking problem, or the
temper, or the tendency to procrastinate! *They* should have to take
the initiative!"

Whenever I hear a spouse make this comment, I try to point out
that fairness isn't the point. What is required to keep a good thing
going, a marriage now being threatened—*this* is the point! And, the
less guilty, or the healthier if you will, is the *logical* one to take the
necessary steps *and* assume a disproportionate share of the burden.
This principle could be described as "the buck stops with the partner best able to carry the load." For example, suppose two people
are hungry. One has plenty of food and the other has little. Decency
and all expectation would require the one with more to give to the

one with less. Or suppose two people are carrying a heavy load. One person is bigger, stronger, and healthier, while the other is small, weak, and injured. Would not the strong person be the logical one to help get the job done by carrying the greater load?

There is an old saying that God or fate has divided the world into two categories: those who have and those who need. Those who are fortunate enough to be among the ones who have should be grateful enough and logical enough to give to those who are in the other category. This is especially true of marriage! The partner who *did not* cause the problem in the marriage is the one who must logically assume the heavier load.

Or, look at this key principle from another angle. Personally, I have never observed a problem in a marriage that did not have two sides! But it is too simple just to say one side is his and one side is hers. What I have found helpful is to see the disruptive problem as having a *causal* side and a *contributive* side. Obviously, one of these will be assigned to him and the other to her, but the two sides of the problem threatening the marriage are causal and contributive.

The *causal* factor can be his or hers and it can be just about anything. It can be alcoholism, a strong habit, perennial bad breath, or a pathological inability to show feeling. The *contributive* factor is always the other partner, who does not know how to handle the *cause* of the marital problem. The contributive partner does not know how to live with an alcoholic or a spouse who has difficulty expressing intimate feelings.

Often a problem in a marriage *begins* with 90 percent being attributable to the mate with the causal factor. At the *beginning* of the problem the contributive mate is a mere 10 percent of the problem. *But,* as the problem develops, that ratio changes from 90–10 to 70–30 to 60–40 to the point that when the problem is really serious we find a rather predictable 50–50! He may have a real drinking problem, in fact this is the *cause* of their marital unrest; but she, by virtue of not knowing how to handle the situation, *contributes* heavily in that at 50–50 she is now driving him to drink! Therefore, the healthier person might just as well take the initiative in healing the situation because, at the point of breakup, they are usually just as guilty as the one who has the problem.

A very important key to keeping a good marriage going is to *take the initiative* in healing the situation. You should especially take the initiative if you are the contributive side of the problem because this probably means you are the healthier and less guilty one. This is not to say there should be dishonesty or a total abdication of one's own rights. This is not to say the causal person should be treated like a child and exempted from any or all responsibility. It is but to say that (1) the stronger person is expected to carry the greater burden, and (2) that it sometimes works wonders to simply admit that the other person might be right.

If you want to fix a bad thing or keep a good thing going, take the initiative!

Key 7: Continually Reevaluate Priorities

This key is equally imperative in keeping a good thing going. There is plenty of evidence, and statistics to burn, indicating that most marriages go bad because many couples today are willing to pay *anything* to acquire *nothing* of real importance, while hoping to obtain the really important values of life at bargain-basement cost.

This was precisely what Soren Kierkegaard, the Danish philosopher and theologian, warned western civilization about in his story of the man who crept into a large department store one night and switched all the price labels. He placed the expensive labels on the inexpensive items and all the cheap tags on the most expensive commodities. Then, when the store opened, customers were able to buy valuable things at little expense but also had to pay exorbitant prices for items of little value.

Smart marriages know this is precisely what our civilization has attempted to do! It has attempted to tell us we can buy the truly luxurious, expensive items like a successful marriage for little or nothing. Our civilization has likewise made us willing to pay anything for commodities of little intrinsic or eternal value.

So real is Kierkegaard's description of our world that droves of unthinking marriages have taken the concept to its next logical step. If things of great value, like a beautiful relationship, can be purchased for nothing, then I can spend all my time and energy buying and accumulating junk. And, if I remain unwilling to pay a high price for the great treasures of life, I can shore up my marriage by accumulating expensive *things*. This is when we say, "What our marriage needs is a color TV ... a new sailboat ..." or *whatever* keeps us from giving our all to the all-important. The result of all this is economic overextension, which is listed by many counselors as the chief cause of divorce in the United States. What are your priorities?

In short, *what* our priorities are, and therefore *where* we are spending our energy, needs constant reevaluation because weak priorities or goals produce weak marriages! It is precisely in marriage the way it is in *faith.* The size of the god you worship has every impact on the size of your personal faith. Having a rinky-dink god tends to produce a rinky-dink faith. If you worship a trite and prejudicial god, you're probably going to have a trite and prejudicial faith. If you worship a great and loving God, you at least have the potential for a great and loving faith!

In the same way, great goals and significant priorities in and for the marriage tend to create potential for a great and significant marriage. If the highest goal (the highest god) in your marriage is accumulating *things,* you simply do not have the hope or potential that the couple enjoys whose *highest* goal is love, togetherness, communication, and purposeful living.

New swimming pools, flashier coats or cars, or a bigger house are not intrinsically wrong. It's just that these things are poor *top priorities.* They are poor compelling gods! Give a first-rate love and energy and sacrifice to a first-rate cause. Know that the truly valuable commodities require the greatest investment. *Then,* it is quite acceptable to give a second-rate love to a second-rate cause. Top priorities that *build* and *nurture* a marriage are God, family, integrity, caring about others, respect. Poor *priorities,* the compelling goals that produce little and cost far too much are things, items and tinseled toys of innumerable variations.

If in your marriage you will constantly reevaluate your priorities and put the important things first, the rewards can be significant. To be disciplined, to reach for the highest one knows is infinitely rewarding. For instance, I have heard marriage counselors report that approximately two in four marriages in this country end in divorce, except among people who go to church or synagogue *regularly!* The record shows that among couples who attend a house of worship regularly the divorce rate changes to one divorce in 500! This has been my observation also, and I mention it here to raise the critical question, if this is so, WHY is it so?

The answer to this question is not to be found in correct theology or the magic of walking through a church door! People who walk through church doors have all the problems known to all other marriages. The difference is, and I've seen it over and over, that couples who go to church or synagogue regularly are more disciplined, are exposed more continuously to the needs of the world, thus minimizing their own problems or greeds, and are regularly exposed to purposes and programs that summon them beyond their own little world. Rather than return to church at age thirty to save their marriage, a very common occurrence, wise couples *order* their priorities and *discipline* their lives and needs by attempting to always pay well for special things that really count and very little for material things that are only nice to have.

Ordered priorities, of which regular worship is but one excellent example, is a critically important key. Dr. Wesley Shrum of Princeton University has done a study on this same subject. Dr. Shrum and his associates interviewed 7,029 people and made some interesting observations. The research group found that couples attending church less than once a year experienced divorce at a rate of 34 percent. Those who attended once to several times a year experience divorce at a rate of 27 percent. Those who attended a house of worship once a month or more had a divorce rate at 18 percent. The correlation is clear. In a much more unscientific way, many years of working with troubled marriages have brought me the same awareness. Personally, I had come to attribute the difference in the odds to disciplined living and ordered priorities.

I believe so very strongly that the great God of the universe, the God of Judeo-Christian history, can and does make such a significant difference in a marriage. I believe, teach, and live that! *But,* what I am trying to say here is that disciplined living and ordered priorities *alone* can make an enormous difference in a marriage. A personal walk with a great and loving God can add *even more* to a relationship, but many couples who are not people of faith are doing so much better than the garden-variety marriage because they are disciplined and ordered.

In keeping a good marriage going it is very important constantly to reevaluate priorities. It is *very* important that a couple discipline themselves to pay the greatest price for the most precious commodities and constantly reevaluate what their compelling, motivating priorities really are.

Key 8: Work At It Together

This entire book is dedicated to the care and maintenance of a good marriage. I have written this book because all of us need to know and many of us want to know what real work is involved if a marriage is to grow and mature. Work, hard work, is inevitable in achieving any great goal and this is especially true in the case of marriage. The only real choice we have is *where* we will deliberately spend our energies! It requires the same energy, degree and kind, to *care* for a marriage, to get out of a marriage, or to start all over in another marriage. Work we must, so why not use all that energy to make the marriage you've got happy and successful!

If we use our energies in this pursuit, then we need to remember that the task of keeping a good thing going, of caring for and maintaining a good marriage, is, of course, a *mutual* task. One partner can do all the right things, take the initiative, develop a sense of humor or all the other important keys, but if *both* are not working at the task *together* there is litle hope for success.

Many people come to my office and say, "Help me! I will do ANYTHING to get her/him to love me again and not leave me!" And, they would do anything. You feel for them. You know how they are hurting and you know from their voice and anguish there is nothing on earth they wouldn't do to save their marriage. It is THIS kind of working TOGETHER that must be done *before* that same energy must be used to save the relationship or to start all over. Work together while that kind of time and effort will spare you from having to use it elsewhere! I tell couples who share their lives with me to work at it just as tenaciously "as you would if you were willing to do anything to get your partner back." Do those things! Work that hard! Do it together and be sure to spend all that energy on the front end of the problem and not on the back.

This need to work together, giving the energy needed to *prevent,* to care and maintain, this is the burden of this entire book. Few of us are naturally disposed in this direction. Our inclination seems to be to coast, hope things work out well, and, if not, then give it everything we've got to *save* it! I'm trying to say, give it everything you've got but give it while there is still time!

I see many people jogging in the city park near my home. They are out in droves, in the heat and in the cold, with great and admirable regimentation. I know many dozens of these young adults.

Many of them are people I have cried with and ached for in my own office. I see them now "getting in shape" so they can appear bright, healthy, attractive, and desirable to someone else. They've lost their first love and are once again hot on the trail of some perfect creature. I think as I see them jogging, *If you had worked that hard to keep what you had, you could be home enjoying the reward. You would not have to be out here working to get back to where you once bailed out.*

All joggers are not guilty of this, of course. Many, like me, are jogging to keep their health and to stay fresh and healthy for the one we have known and loved for so many years. And, while I jog, my wife gets her exercise by walking briskly around the block. Occasionally we will run into each other at the corner. We stop, speak, and laugh. Neither of us says, "Hi! We're out caring for our good marriage!" But, each of us knows that each of us is out there for the other and for ourselves. We know that our effort to stay physically healthy is just another example of the two of us working at keeping a good thing going and working at it together.

Do the work the two of you would have to do if you wanted to save the marriage or if you had to begin again. Why is it that we will do anything to correct a problem that we won't do anything to prevent? *Working together* we can make that truism a blatant lie! We can, with forethought and determination, do everything to prevent a problem we don't want to waste the same energy on having to correct.

Working at it together, *now,* may mean planning or plotting. It may occasionally entail healthy confrontation or heavy discussion. Working at it may mean dialogue and even détente concerning some subjects or conflicts. Working at it together may mean many things, clear or unclear, vague or in focus, but it always means *working* and doing it together!

Unfortunately, most of us don't like work. We avoid it when we can. We hope to find a union that is both automatically great and conspicuously nondemanding. But, no such marriage exists that does not demand work and maturation. No matter how we may rationalize our disdain for a demanding, though rewarding, relationship, this truth will ultimately shine through.

For success in marriage you mustn't have a lottery mentality—putting in as little as possible, hoping to hit the jackpot. Instead, think of life as a solid investment from which you receive dividends in terms of what you put in. Work at care and maintenance. And, do it together.

Don't Run By What You're Trying to Catch Up With!

A good marriage does require care and maintenance. We don't just stumble into a perfect relationship that requires no growth or struggle. We are not going to find a relationship that is eternally exciting and constantly reassuring. As I wrote in the beginning of this book, we are going to find, no matter how hard we look or where we look, that *everyone* is hard to live with. We are going to find that the only real difference is that some partners give each other enough good things in return to make it all worthwhile. Consequently, we may learn to stay with what we've got rather than enter that painful world where we look back and yearn for the return of what is lost.

Your attitude toward marriage may well be similar to that of the farmer who had grown tired of working his land. He decided to sell the place and move to another part of the country that seemed more attractive and challenging. He proceeded to put the property into the hands of a real estate agent. The agent inspected the place and the next day came by with a proposed advertisement. The advertisement told about the lovely old farmhouse set on ninety acres of rolling countryside—fertile, scenic, and fashionable. The write-up went on in glowing terms about the advantages of the house and land and location. The farmer read the description, thought a moment, and tore it up, saying "I've been looking for a place just like that all my life. You don't think I'd let you sell it now that I've found it, do you?"

You may also find that your marriage, as with all good things, simply needs care and maintenance, love, appreciation, affirmation, and hard work. You may simply need to recall Fra Giovanni's statement: "No peace lies in the future that is not hidden in the present."